Property Rights

Terry L. Anderson and Laura E. Huggins

PROPERTY RIGHTS

A Practical Guide to Freedom and Prosperity

HOOVER INSTITUTION PRESS
Stanford University   Stanford, California

www.hoover.org

Hoover Institution Press Publication No. 515
Copyright © 2003 by the Board of Trustees of the
    Leland Stanford Junior University

First printing 2003
09   08   07   06   05   04   03   9   8   7   6   5   4   3   2   1

Manufactured in the United States of America
The paper used in this publication meets the minimum requirements
of American National Standard for Information Sciences—Permanence
of Paper for Printed Library Materials, ANSI Z39.48-1984. ⊚

Library of Congress Cataloging-in-Publication Data
Anderson, Terry Lee, 1946–
    Property rights : a practical guide to freedom and prosperity /
by Terry L. Anderson and Laura E. Huggins.
        p.   cm.
    Includes bibliographical references and index.
    ISBN 0-8179-3912-1 (alk. paper)
    1. Property.   2. Real property.   3. Right of property.   4. Liberty.
5. Economic development.   I. Huggins, Laura E., 1976–
II. Title.
HB701 .A44   2003
323.4′6—dc21   2002038883

CONTENTS

FOREWORD

A number of organized Hoover Initiatives are under way at the Hoover Institution. These initiatives represent multiyear sustained efforts in which Hoover fellows and other prominent scholars focus on specific and important topics pertaining to our mission. One of these important initiatives is Property Rights, the Rule of Law, and Economic Performance.

Property rights are currently threatened by a variety of state, national, and international forces, yet property rights are seldom discussed in the world of public policy. Do we take our property rights for granted in society? Is the American public aware of possible entrenchments on and erosion of our system of property rights? The Hoover Institution judges that it is important to raise these issues as part of a diverse and widespread public dialogue. Thus, we have embarked on a path that focuses on the benefits to be preserved from observing and protecting property rights and that articulates these concepts to a broad audience using language that is absent of jargon and less esoteric. Our goal is to publish and disseminate ideas to the public, the media, lawmakers, and others in order to address this important public policy issue and encourage positive policy formation by converting conceptual insights into practical initiatives judged to be beneficial to society.

The Property Rights initiative was formally launched in spring 2000 with a conference, held at Hoover, around the topic "The

Law and Economics of Property Rights." Organized by Terry Anderson, the Martin and Illie Anderson Senior Fellow at Hoover, and Fred McChesney, professor of law at Northwestern University, the conference explored ongoing legal and economic issues surrounding property rights, which led to the production of an important academic book, *Property Rights: Cooperation, Conflict, and Law* (Princeton University Press, 2003). In addition to this major scholarly offering, I am pleased to present *Property Rights: A Practical Guide to Freedom and Prosperity*. This primer conveys the important but sometimes complex concepts surrounding the study of property rights in an easily understood and straightforward fashion.

The Property Rights initiative, and this book specifically, is made possible by the significant support of Peter and Kirsten Bedford. I thank them for sponsoring this important initiative and acknowledge their sustained interest over two decades. Peter has also served as a member of Hoover's Board of Overseers during much of this time, contributing to the strategic direction and intellectual health of the Institution.

I also hasten to thank my colleagues Terry Anderson and Laura Huggins, who agreed to author this crucial piece of the outcome of the conference. This is a topic that deserves attention beyond the experts. As citizens, we need to be aware of the importance of these matters in preserving our freedom and promoting our well-being as a society. I truly feel that the Anderson-Huggins effort is a superb step forward in this regard.

John Raisian
Director
Hoover Institution

ACKNOWLEDGMENTS

In spring 2000, the Hoover Institution embarked on a research initiative that focuses on the benefits to be gained from protecting and promoting property rights. A conference was held to help launch the initiative and further explore the importance of property rights. Participants included many of the world's top property rights scholars. The papers from that conference were edited by Terry L. Anderson and Fred S. McChesney and compiled in *Property Rights: Cooperation, Conflict, and Law* (2003). We would especially like to thank P. J. Hill and Fred S. McChesney, both of whom contributed to the conference and to the forthcoming volume, for their comments on earlier drafts and to thank all of the other contributors for their scholarship, which we drew upon for this book: Yoram Barzel, Louis De Alessi, Harold Demsetz, Thráinn Eggertsson, Richard Epstein, William Fischel, David Haddock, Gary Libecap, Dean Lueck, Ed West, and Bruce Yandle. We are also appreciative of Stephen Langlois of the Hoover Institution for his remarks on the manuscript. Projects such as this require idea entrepreneurs—for this we owe a special thanks to John Raisian, director of the Hoover Institution.

INTRODUCTION

Consider the prospect of investing in land. In the United States, we take the security of such an investment for granted, but in other countries that security is not always available. For example, though Zimbabwe has a constitution forbidding the confiscation of land without compensation, so-called land reform is taking land from people who thought they had secure title and giving it to others. As a result of this land redistribution, productivity is down and people are starving. Furthermore, citizens are being persecuted and killed. This is not to say that the distribution of land ownership is necessarily just in countries such as Zimbabwe, but it does emphasize that security of property rights is crucial to freedom and prosperity.

This book argues that property rights are central to freedom and prosperity. It is easy to see this in the case of title to land as contrasted between the United States and Zimbabwe. The same point holds for all property rights. Be it property rights to one's self (human capital), one's investments (physical capital), or one's ideas (intellectual capital), secure claims to assets give people the ability to make their own decisions, reaping the benefits of good choices and bearing the costs of bad ones.

The necessary link between freedom and prosperity is perhaps well illustrated with slavery, which necessarily eliminates the possibility of freedom for those in bondage. If individuals do not own themselves, they cannot be free. The same holds for assets other than one's self. When individuals invest in goods and those investments are threatened by takings, freedom is diminished and prosperity will decline.

The idea that property rights provide the foundation for a free society has long been understood. Protection of private property was of utmost importance to the people of England who penned the Magna Carta and to the Founding Fathers of the United States who drafted the Declaration of Independence and the Constitution. In the latter case, they had just fought the Revolutionary War, which resulted from the Crown's abuse of colonial property rights, as evidenced in the original slogan of the revolution: "Liberty, property, and no stamps!" (See Bowen 1966.)

Since the American Revolution, the United States has experienced economic growth and individual freedoms unsurpassed in world history. We have seen per capita incomes approximately double every forty years, we have eliminated slavery, and we have created tremendous possibilities for geographic, social, and economic mobility.

Despite living in an era of triumphant capitalism, however, property rights are still threatened by a variety of state, national, and international forces. A case in point: The U.S. Supreme Court recently dealt the protection of property rights a significant legal setback in *Tahoe-Sierra Preservation Council Inc. v. Tahoe Regional Planning Agency*, 535 U.S. 040 (2002). The court sided against the landowners by claiming that a development moratorium lasting several years was not a compensable taking and thus the property owners were not entitled to compensation for losses in property value caused by the regulatory restrictions.

The real question in this case was who should pay to maintain Lake Tahoe, all of us who enjoy its beauty or only those unlucky few who used their savings to buy development lots? Justice

Holmes answered this question some eighty years ago in *Pennsyl-vania Coal v. Mahon*, 260 U.S. 393 (1922), when he explained that "a strong public desire to improve the public condition is not enough to warrant achieving the desire by a shorter cut than the constitutional way of paying for the change" (quoted in Adler 2002). Though this case pales when compared with takings by tyrannical governments such as the one ruling Zimbabwe, it illus-trates the necessity of vigilance and the necessity of understanding the nexus between secure property rights and a free society.

The crucial connection among secure property rights, free-dom, and prosperity is elucidated in this primer. We describe what property rights are (chapter 1), what they do (chapter 2), how they evolve (chapter 3), how they can be protected (chapter 4), and what their future might be (chapter 5). We emphasize that this is a primer, a brief treatment of a vast and complex subject studied by scholars from many disciplines. You will find discus-sions of philosophers, political thinkers, economists, and lawyers. We highlight that our intent is not to cover all of the intricacies of the subject, but rather to give nonexperts a blueprint for how societies can encourage or discourage freedom and prosperity through their property rights institutions.

This primer might be thought of as the *Reader's Digest* version of a much longer treatment of property rights, *Property Rights: Cooperation, Conflict, and Law*, edited by Terry L. Anderson and Fred S. McChesney (2003). The book began as a conference at the Hoover Institution, which brought together lawyers, econo-mists, and political scientists to discuss our modern understanding of the law and economics of property rights. From the conference, the scholars refined their thoughts into chapters and combined them into what is one of the most definitive volumes on the sub-ject. For the reader who wants to go beyond this primer, we have referenced chapters in the longer volume that will provide greater depth for the points discussed here.

Much of the literature on property rights—and this primer is no exception—relies on lessons from history. We have used many examples from the United States frontier, where new resources, expanding populations, emerging technologies, and a lack of formal government afforded a crucible for property rights evolution and institutional innovation.

Despite their being from history, these important lessons are no less applicable to the study of property rights today. From the open access of the oceans to the far reaches of space, new frontiers where property rights are undefined offer new opportunities for their evolution. The genetic structure of living organisms serves as an example of such a frontier.

Consider the following hypothetical case (Stix 2002). A man named Salvador Dolly gives blood for a genetic test to determine his fitness to father a child. The testing company sells the remains of Dolly's blood to NuGenEra, a biotechnology company. Nu-GenEra discovers that Dolly's genes make him resistant to HIV. The company quickly applies for a patent on his genome. When Dolly finds out that his genes guard against the deadly virus, he sets up a company to market his blood. NuGenEra sues Dolly for patent infringement, claiming that it owns his genome. Will Dolly have to forgo property rights to his own genome? Should these rights be balanced against society's need for the therapies for HIV? This case brings to light just some of the many unanswered questions regarding how the "genomics" era may affect intellectual property rights.

How we have dealt with the evolution and protection of property rights in the past and how we deal with them as they are applied to new issues in the future will determine how free and prosperous our society is. If we allow individuals more autonomy in the use of their human and physical property, they will have an incentive to invest in their assets and to use them more productively. These incentives result if people are, as the Nobel laureate

Milton Friedman titled one of his books, "free to choose." We hope this primer helps readers better understand what property rights are and how important they are to freedom, an asset that is all too precious and scarce.

CHAPTER ONE

What Are Property Rights?

PROPERTY RIGHTS: The right to life is the source of all rights—and the right to property is their only implementation. Without property rights, no other rights are possible. Since man has to sustain his life by his own effort, the man who has no right to the product of his effort has no means to sustain his life. The man who produces while others dispose of his product is a slave.

Ayn Rand, *The Virtue of Selfishness*

ANYONE WHO has observed children quarreling knows that disputes occur when the rules are not clear. They may be fighting over who has the right to a toy; how much time must be given to hide in a game of hide-and-seek; or who will call a foul in a basketball game. Experienced adults address these disputes by defining the rules of the game—who has the right to do what and when.

Just as children need rights resolution for harmonious play, so is rights resolution a necessary condition for life in a civil society. Imagine a world wherein nobody can identify who owns what and the rules that govern property vary from person to person (DeSoto 2000, 15). Chaos far worse than children quar-reling would ensue. As philosopher Thomas Hobbes stated, life in a world of anarchy without rules and property rights would be "nasty, brutish, and short" (Leviathan 1985, 186).

To avoid anarchy, citizens create order by agreeing on rules that specify who can do what, who reaps the benefits from pro-ductive activity, and who bears the costs of disruptive activity. These rules are the essence of property rights. Property refers to much more than just real estate. Property rights determine who may cultivate a field, who can park in which slot in a parking lot, who is responsible for pollution, and who can profit from the sale of music. If property rights are clearly defined and enforced, cooperation replaces conflict as property owners bargain with one another and share in gains from trade.

This primer explores what property rights are, how they en-courage civility and economic progress, how they evolve and de-volve, how they can be taken by others, how barriers can help protect them, and whether they will be preserved in the future.

Who Can Do What?

Property rights are the rules of the game that determine who gets to do what and who must compensate whom if damages occur. Return to the scene of the children quarreling. Disputes over toys result when ownership is unclear and are resolved by clarifying which child has the right to the toy. Children can play a peaceful game of hide-and-seek as long as it is clear who hides and who seeks, where hiding can occur, how much time must be allotted for hiding, and so on. Similarly, when property lines between land parcels are clear, disputes are far fewer, hence the familiar adage "Good fences make good neighbors." Patents and copyrights make clear who profits from intellectual capital. Trespass and nuisance laws hold responsible those who encroach on another's property.

Property rights may be established as formally as filing a deed with a court or as informally as acknowledging a first come, first served rule for allocating seats at a movie theater. They govern access to tangible assets, such as cars and parcels of land, but they also apply to less tangible assets, such as patents and copyrights.

Whether they are formal or informal, whether they apply to tangible or intangible assets, property rights consist of multiple characteristics often referred to by lawyers as a bundle of sticks, each of which represents a different aspect of property ownership. These ownership characteristics include the right to use (and so to profit from) an asset, the right to exclude others from using the asset, and the right to transfer the asset to others. In its most complete form, ownership of property grants the owner control of all the sticks as long as use does not infringe on the rights of others. The owner of a car, for example, has the right to carry friends and family in the car, as long as he or she drives it in a manner that does not endanger other drivers. Property rights allow the owner to determine the uses of the asset and to derive value from the asset. They also ensure the owner of the rights to physically transform and even destroy the asset.

Property rights also come in less complete packages, allowing an owner to derive only partial value from an asset, to exclude only some users, or to transfer only certain uses for only a specified time period. Returning to the case of a car, an owner is often restricted from using it as a taxi unless licensed to do so. In the case of land, zoning regulations may limit the uses of specified parcels no matter what the landowner might want.

Even if property rights are defined, they must be enforced if they are to be effective. Consider the importance of clearly specified and enforced rules in a basketball game. During the game, property rights to space on the court belong to the first player to occupy it, and those rights cannot be invaded. If they are, a foul has occurred. However, interpreting whether the space was already occupied before it was entered by another requires a referee to make the judgment calls and enforce the rights.

Similarly, property rights rules that govern civil interaction must be defined and enforced. Boundary disputes between landowners can arise because survey lines are not clear. If a tree branch grows across a boundary line, does the invasion of space above the ground constitute a violation of property rights? If music from a stereo or smoke from a chimney crosses a neighbor's property line, does this violate the neighbor's property rights? Answering such questions requires institutions of adjudication, such as courts, that serve the same purpose as the referee—defining and enforcing property rights. Before further expanding the definition of property rights, it is important to look back to what people thought of property rights in the past and to touch on how these thoughts were implemented in everyday life.

Philosophical Evolution

On a philosophical level, property rights have interested scholars at least since the time of Plato and Aristotle. Plato's *Republic* presents his vision of the ideal society, one devoid of belongings. Plato argued that property should be communal both in ownership and use. He believed that the rulers of a city should not own property so that they would not tear the city in pieces by differing over "mine" and "not mine" (Pipes 1999, 6).

Aristotle's *Politics* challenged Plato's vision, posing the question, "What should be our arrangements about property: should the citizens of the perfect state have their possessions in common or not?" He concludes that property should be owned privately because "that which is common to the greatest number has the least care bestowed upon it" (Aristotle *Politics* 1. 8–11).

Early Catholic church theorists followed Aristotle's lead. Thomas Aquinas established the church's definitive position in his *Summa Theologica*, arguing that private property rights were legitimate within a grander system of natural law—orderly principles that govern the functioning of nature. He argued that common ownership promoted neither efficiency nor harmony, instead causing costly discord. He believed that, for humans to perfect themselves spiritually, they need the security provided by ownership.

With the rise of Protestantism, enlightenment scholars such as John Locke continued to examine the boundaries of property rights. In *The Second Treatise on Government* (1690), Locke argued that property rights existed prior to (and thus with or without) government and that these rights were derived from natural rights, such as the right to one's own life and liberty. According to Locke, if a man owns his own labor, he should also own the fruits of that labor. By Locke's definition, ownership of a thing must include the right to use that thing and retain gains from its use. The protection of these natural rights is the primary justification for the existence of government. As Locke stated, "The great and chief end therefore of men uniting into commonwealths, and putting themselves under government, is the preservation of property." Locke also argued that if a ruler violates any of his subjects' property rights he is "at war" with them, and therefore the ruler may be disobeyed (Bethell 1998, 16).

Locke's perspective influenced Adam Smith's work, especially *The Wealth of Nations* (1776), a century later. Smith built on Locke's view that property existed within a larger system of natural rights and that the institutions of property and government were self-reinforcing. Private property, according to Smith, created a role for government in defending property, and the existence of government created the security to stimulate the creation of new property.

Smith built on the relationship between property and government to justify government's role in providing national defense and in administering justice. National defense seeks to protect property from external threats, while the administration of justice ensures the integrity of property rights in the face of internal disputes. He argued that these two functions are critical to the sanctity of private ownership and ultimately to determining the wealth of nations.

Property Rights Through History

Practical consideration of the benefits of property rights doubtlessly preceded the scholarly inquiries, and lessons regarding the centrality of private ownership in establishing orderly and efficient societies are still being learned today. Studies of primitive cultures conclude that property rights were a central part of people's existence. In fact, there is no record in anthropological studies of societies that were unaware of property rights (Pipes 1999, 116).

The existence of property rights from primitive times to the present is best explained by a human desire for order, or perhaps for the benefits that order conferred. In a seminal article describing the problems that arise when resources are not privately owned, but are common to all, H. Scott Gordon (1954) concluded:

> Stable primitive cultures appear to have discovered the dangers of common property tenure and to have developed measures to protect their resources. Or if a more Darwinian explanation be preferred, we may say that only those primitive cultures have survived which succeeded in developing such institutions. (134–35)

For much of human history, when hunting and gathering were

the principal forms of economic activity, claims of tribal owner-ship applied to control of territory, while individual property claims included weapons, tools, and other personal belongings (Pipes 1999, 12). Pre- and post-Columbian Indians understood the importance of property rights and designed institutions that clarified who had rights to land, hunting territories, and personal property. Because agricultural lands had to be improved through the investment of time and effort, they were often privately owned. The Mahican Indians, for example, possessed hereditary rights to use well-defined tracts of fertile land along rivers. The Hopi tribes marked off territory by boundary stones engraved with symbols of the clan (Anderson 1996, 6). Personal items such as the teepee, which were costly to produce, were privately owned as well (Anderson 1995).

The importance of property rights increased as societies shifted from a hunter-gatherer existence to an agrarian lifestyle, in which economic activity focused on territory and soil cultiva-tion. One of the earliest examples of property rights attached to agricultural lands comes from ancient Greece. Farmers who la-bored for themselves were exempt from paying tribute to aristo-crats. This economic independence became a guarantee of free-dom, so Greeks were motivated to acquire property. They were further motivated to protect their acquisition because if a Greek lost his land, he also lost his rights of citizenship (Pipes 1996, 100).

With population growth came competition for territory and other natural resources. Individuals sought confirmation that they would be rewarded for investing in the land; they wanted the security that someone else could not confiscate the wealth they created. As a result, pressures on the state to guarantee the se-curity of ownership increased. In 1215, King John of England agreed to the demands of his barons and authorized the Magna Carta. This influential charter protected property owners against the powers of central government. David Hume in his *History of*

England wrote that the Magna Carta provided for the equal distribution of justice and the free enjoyment of property. Both provisions were "the great objects for which political society was at first founded by men, which the people have a perpetual and unalienable right to recall, and which not time, nor precedent, nor statute, nor positive institution, ought to deter them from keeping ever upmost in their thoughts and attention" (1778, 445).

By the sixteenth century, it was clear that the crown's authority stopped where private property began. The ideas of individual sovereignty and individual proprietorship became entrenched in the common law of Britain and subsequently in the Constitution of the United States.

Just as hunting and gathering gave way to settled agriculture, settled agriculture gave way to the industrial revolution. That transition required secure property rights to capital assets in order to guarantee private investors a return on their investments. The rise of contractual arrangements such as the modern corporation and the growth of impersonal markets depended on protection of capital from governments by constitutions and from fellow men by civil laws (Pipes 1999, 44).

The authors of the U.S. Declaration of Independence and Constitution shared Locke's and Smith's beliefs in the importance of private ownership. The Founding Fathers firmly believed that the human right to private property had to be protected in law as the basis for individual liberty, a free society, and a free economy. The Fifth Amendment to the Constitution, for example, was aimed at protecting private property from governmental takings. Because the rule of law and constitutions guaranteed the sanctity of property in England and the United States during the eighteenth and nineteenth centuries, trade and commerce flourished and economies grew.

During that time period, however, increasing numbers of people called for state regulation and the abolition of property. Critics of capitalism argued that it was destroying social equality. In the *Communist Manifesto* (1848), for example, Friederick Engels and Karl Marx denounced private property as exclusively a product of capitalism. Accordingly, they claimed that "the theory of the communist may be summed up in a single sentence: abolition of private property."

If ever there was a dramatic example of the importance of private ownership of labor, land, and capital, it was the economic performance of communist regimes. Lacking the incentives inherent in private ownership, the Soviet Union and its satellites stagnated or declined to the point that they had no choice but to reform their economic systems.

By the time the Berlin Wall fell and communism collapsed, it was obvious to most observers that private property rights and their definition and enforcement by the rule of law were necessary ingredients for economic growth. Since the 1980s, many countries have transferred assets and rights from the public sector to private ownership in an attempt to improve efficiency. Industries undergoing privatization around the world include transportation, telecommunications, airlines, banking, mining, natural gas, and electric power (see Megginson, Nash, van Randeborgh 1996, 115).

An Economic Perspective

As the economic scales were tipping in favor of private ownership and away from communism, law and economics scholars were refining their explanations of how property rights work to encourage productivity and of the consequences of abrogating property rights. The work of Nobel laureate Ronald Coase and other economists such as Harold Demsetz and Armen Alchian have provided a more general approach to why property rights have emerged. These theories, according to Alan Ryan, suggest that "property comes into existence under the impulse of pressures towards efficiency through a process parallel to that of natural selection" (Pipes 1999, 63). Nobel laureate Douglass North argues that economic growth occurs when secure property rights exist to make it worthwhile to invest in socially productive activity. He relies on historical examples to demonstrate that societies built on private ownership and the rule of law are more likely to experience economic development.

The economics of property rights focuses on individuals as the basic unit of analysis (for a complete discussion, see Anderson and McChesney 2003). Accordingly, a group or society is an aggregation of individual preferences and procedures. Building on the individual as the unit of analysis, four basic tenets guide the economics of property rights.

First, individuals make choices under conditions of scarcity. The choices people make are constrained because resources are limited. In a world of scarcity, one use of an asset precludes another. For example, water used for irrigation cannot provide a free-flowing stream in which fish can spawn. Land used for subdivisions cannot provide wilderness amenities, and so on.

Second, individuals act rationally to pursue their self-interests by adjusting to the benefits and costs of their actions. Rationality means that people have well-defined preferences and act systematically to maximize their well-being subject to their wealth and income constraints. Because resources are not limitless, rational maximization requires individuals to weigh the benefits and costs of their choices. As we shall see later, the rationality tenet is particularly important in thinking about how property rights evolve because rational actors will work to define and enforce property rights only if the benefits of doing so exceed the cost.

Rational maximization in the face of resource scarcity leads to the third principle, namely that individuals will compete for control of scarce resources and that the nature of the competition will depend on the rules of the game. Consider the example of scarce movie theater seats. If the demand for seats exceeds the supply and the price of seats does not rise to reflect this excess demand, people will queue to get the seats. Alternatively, if the seat price rises, those who value the seats more highly will compete by paying more. Similarly, American Indians competed with early European settlers for scarce land. When the two sides agreed on the property rights, they traded with one another, as the famous exchange of trinkets and beads for Manhattan Island illustrates. When the rights to land were less clear, however, as in the case of nomadic Plains tribes, and when the European settlers had a standing army press their interests, competition for land took the form of fighting rather than bargaining. Racing for theater seats or fighting for western lands are costly forms of competition because of the time, effort, and resources expended in the process.

The final tenet is that well-specified and transferable property rights encourage gains from trade. Racing and fighting waste valuable time and money. Therefore, individuals and groups have an incentive to develop property rights and encourage exchange. With property rights well defined and transferable, owners have an incentive to husband the resource because they capture the future value of conservation. If owners do not put a private resource to its highest and best use, others who see the waste can offer to buy it and improve on its use. For these reasons, private ownership replaces the waste of racing and fighting with more efficient long-term use. Instead of people rushing to catch fish and in the process depleting fish populations, owners with fishing rights are more likely to harvest on a sustainable basis (De Alessi 2003). When water can be freely drawn from a stream, there is a race to the pump house. On the other hand, if water rights are well-specified and transferable, owners have an incentive to conserve the precious resource (see Anderson and Snyder 1995).

Conclusion

The four tenets described above guide the analysis of property rights that follows. In chapter 2, we elaborate on how property rights encourage efficient use of scarce resources, offering numerous empirical examples to compare private ownership with alternative institutional arrangements. The examples document the positive impact property rights have on resource stewardship, human cooperation, and wealth.

If private property is generally a superior institution, it is important to understand the rules by which property rights are defined and enforced. In chapter 3, we consider the evolution of property rights by introducing the institutional entrepreneur who recognizes gains from moving resources from open access to private ownership. After realizing the possibility of higher-valued uses for an asset, the entrepreneur must define and enforce property rights to capture the higher values.

Government may be the cheapest way of defining and enforcing property rights, but it is naive to assume that government, with its monopoly on force, is always the optimal solution. In chapter 4, we raise the fundamental question of political economy: When collective coercive power is necessary to enforce property rights and the rule of law, how can it be constrained from taking and redistributing property rights, especially without compensation to the property holder?

The efficacy of property rights and free societies depends on our ability to build and maintain barriers against takings. In chapter 5, we discuss the future of property rights and the new frontiers for the evolution of property rights. Here we hope to stimulate the reader to find new applications of the property rights approach.

CHAPTER TWO

What Do Property Rights Do?

It is precisely those things which belong to "the people" which have historically been despoiled—wild creatures, the air, and waterways being notable examples. This goes to the heart of why property rights are socially important in the first place. Property rights mean self-interested monitors. No owned creatures are in danger of extinction. No owned forests are in danger of being leveled. No one kills the goose that lays the golden egg when it is his goose.

Thomas Sowell, *Knowledge and Decisions*

MOST DISPUTES among young children result from disagreements over ownership of important assets such as toys. When the use of a toy is questioned, it is because ownership claims, even if temporary, are unclear. In some cases, quarreling may even turn into violence. To resolve the conflict and avoid violence, a child instinctively seeks to define rights by claiming the toy as "mine."

The cause of disputes among children is the same one that has caused conflicts between individuals, tribes, and nations throughout history, namely, scarcity. If we did not face scarcity, there would be no reason for disagreements over possesions such as toys because everyone would have as much as he or she wanted.

However, as Thomas Sowell (2001, 2) explains, "there has never been enough to satisfy everyone completely. This is the real constraint. That is what scarcity means." Scarcity dictates that there are competing uses for valuable assets, whether those assets are natural or man-made.

How competition for use of a scarce resource is resolved depends on whether property rights are well defined, well enforced, and readily transferable. In the absence of these three dimensions, conflict results because people do not know who has the right to the property in question, what the boundaries of the rights are, and whether they can trade with one another to resolve their competing demands. If property rights are not well defined and enforced, their value is up for grabs and people fight for use of the property rather than find ways of cooperating.

Without property rights, people race to capture valuable assets or expend precious time and effort fighting over ownership. Racing is well illustrated by open access to fisheries, when fishers must be first to catch the fish lest it is caught by others. Leaving a fish to grow larger or to reproduce is the equivalent of leaving money on the table for others to take. If one fisher does not take a fish, another will, with fish stocks possibly reduced to the point where populations are unsustainable. This explains why the Food and Agricultural Organization of the United Nations finds that 25 percent of the commercial fish stocks in the world are overfished. Similarly, in a 1998 report to the U.S. Congress, the National Marine Fisheries Service categorized ninety fish stocks in United States water as overfished and ten stocks as approaching overfished conditions.

The rush to claim Internet addresses illustrates another case of racing. Domain name space was initially seen as a public resource, leading to confusion over ownership. Companies discovered quickly that they had to race to secure their Internet identities, often only to discover that those names had already been claimed. Squabbling broke out and cybersquatters and cyberpirates became prevalent. Fighting over resources diverts resources away from consumption and investments in new assets and toward efforts to take or defend. The worst example of fighting over property rights is war wherein "to the victor go the spoils" (see Haddock 2003).

History has shown that cooperation will replace racing and conflict if property rights are well defined, enforced, and transferable. Definition of the property and the rights of its owner clarifies who can enjoy and benefit from the property. It determines who is in control. Enforcement means that those who do not own the property (or lack permission from its owner) are unable to use the property or capture benefits from it. Well-defined and enforced property rights also guarantee that the owner reaps the rewards from good stewardship and bears the costs of poor stewardship. Finally, transferability means the owner will take into account the values of other potential users. If another user values a resource more highly than the current owner and offers to purchase it, the two have an incentive to cooperate in order to realize the gains available from trade.

The Tragedy of the Commons

The phenomenon of racing and fighting to capture valuable resources in the absence of well-defined and enforced property rights is termed *the tragedy of the commons* (Hardin 1968). The phrase derives from the incentive to overgraze pastures that are open to all grazers. Each potential grazer has an incentive to fatten his livestock on the grass before someone else gets it. Open access to resources lacks two critical components that property rights systems share—exclusion and governance. Without these two components, people have little incentive to economize on the use of resources. Rather, the incentive is to overuse the asset before someone else does (see Eggertsson 2003).

The first inhabitants of this continent faced the tragedy of the commons in many instances. Indeed, anthropologist Paul Martin (1984) believes that the extinction of the mammoth, the mastodon, the ground sloth, and the saber-toothed cat was, directly or indirectly, related to "prehistoric overkill," which was a manifestation of this tragedy. With no one owning the prehistoric animals, hunters had no incentive to conserve them. Evidence suggests that Plains Indians overharvested big game such as elk and deer when there was competition among tribes, possibly explaining the dearth of wildlife found by the Lewis and Clark expedition when it crossed the Continental Divide.

Indians might have similarly decimated bison populations on the plains if they had had the technology (namely, rifles) to do so and had the demand for the hides, leather, and meat. What they lacked, however, the Europeans did not. Two hundred years ago, 30 million to 70 million bison roamed the western plains, but by 1895 only some 800 remained—most in captivity on private ranches. With hunting open to all, commercial hide hunters, settlers, and thrill seekers shot millions of bison. The massacre continued until bison were nearly driven to extinction, and complete extinction was averted because entrepreneurs saw value in taking the necessary effort to capture some animals and protect them as private property.

Finally, consider pumping from an oil pool or a groundwater basin (see Libecap 2003). Like several children drinking with straws from the same soda, each pumper has an incentive to pump fast, leaving less oil or water for other pumpers. The children might suffer a headache if they drink too fast, and oil pumpers suffer the cost of not getting as much oil from the pool as they could if they pumped more slowly over a longer term. Groundwater pumpers suffer the cost of having to sink their wells deeper, of having salt water intrude, and of having land subside when wells are depleted.

Escaping Tragedy

Interestingly, the number of actual cases of the tragedy of the commons prevailing to the point of complete extinction or exhaustion of a resource is small. Some examples of animals reaching extinction include the passenger pigeon and the dodo bird. What is it that stops the tragedy from going to the limit?

The number is small because people recognize the tragedy before it is too late and devise exclusion and governance rules that can prevent racing and fighting. As long as the supply is large in comparison to demand, as it was, for example, in the early days of bison hunting, there is no reason to expend effort trying to define and enforce property rights. But as resources become more scarce, individuals have an incentive to restrict access and prevent complete exhaustion of the resource. In the next chapter, we take up the question of what determines when and how people go about excluding others from the commons to prevent tragedy. Here, we simply describe three main institutions that are used to restrict access to resources and hence discourage the tragedy of the commons.

Community Commons

One way to escape the tragedy of the commons is for the people who are competing for a valuable resource to join together as a community for the purpose of excluding others and establishing governance rules. The users solve the open access problem by limiting access only to community members. Common property regimes are halfway houses between a completely open access commons and full private rights. They can be a practical solution when an asset is valuable enough to justify the costs of organizing the group, but not valuable enough to justify the effort necessary to precisely divide the asset into private, transferable rights (see De Alessi 2003).

On the western frontier, cattlemen's associations established communal rights. Because it was costly to specifically define land boundaries in the absence of surveys and to confine cattle prior to the invention of barbed wire, cattlemen organized into associations that limited access to the grazing commons. Their associations declared when a range was fully stocked and closed the range to new entrants. Though they had no formal, legal claim to the land, the community of cattlemen enforced their claims by excluding newcomers from roundups and by threatening violence if necessary. As we shall see in chapter 3, the invention of barbed wire changed the cost of establishing private, transferable grazing rights.

The Swiss city of Torbel provides another example of communal land ownership that is centuries old. Torbel is a village of approximately 600 people. It has five types of communally owned property: alpine grazing meadows, forests, waste lands, irrigation systems, and paths and roads connecting privately and communally owned properties. The village rules are voted on by all citizens, determining who has access to the commons and what can be done with the land, the water, and the timber. Once communal rights are established, they are strictly defined and enforced. For example, the "wintering rule" states that no citizen can send more cows to the alpine meadows than he can feed during the winter. An official levies a fine on those who exceed quotas and is allowed to keep one half of the fines for himself. The success of Torbel's system has largely been due to the small number of individuals involved and their longstanding traditions (Ostrom 1990).

For several reasons, however, communal systems do not completely eliminate the tragedy of the commons. Depending on the size and cohesiveness of the community, conflicts over who has what rights may remain. How many cows can each cattleman graze, how much timber can each Swiss villager cut, and how many fish can each fisher catch? Furthermore, suppose a community member grazes too many cows, cuts too much wood, or catches too many fish. What are the enforcement sanctions against the community members? As long as the community is small and homogeneous, defining and enforcing communal rights is relatively easy, but as group size and heterogeneity increase, it is harder to monitor what each member is doing, thus making it easier to get away with taking more from the commons.

Communal forms of ownership also make it more difficult to take advantage of gains from trade. Any individual member of the community may find it advantageous to sell his or her share of the communal resource, but this potentially erodes group homogeneity. That is why communal shares are not usually transferable, and if they are, why transferability often requires group approval.

Mutual irrigation ditches provide a good example of these problems. The amount of water to which each irrigator is entitled may be clear, but because monitoring use is costly, irrigators may take more than their allotted share. Communal management is further complicated by the fact that users share in the operation and maintenance of the ditch. If any one member shirks responsibilities, the other members will bear additional operation and maintenance costs. Community norms and customs can reduce the propensity of members to take too much water or evade their operation and maintenance responsibilities, but this requires maintaining group homogeneity. As a result, shares in mutual ditch companies are not simply transferable, especially if the potential transferee is a newcomer who may not share the community values.

Private Property

Communal forms of ownership often evolve into private property rights. The move from communal rights that exclude outsiders and specify communal rules to private property rights requires more precision in the definition and enforcement of rights and allows the individual owner to decide whether or not to transfer ownership. Definition makes it clear which individuals have what rights; enforcement guarantees exclusion of all other potential users; and transferability forces the owner to consider the value of alternative uses. Hence, private property rights give owners the incentive to maintain their assets and to seek higher-valued uses for them.

William Bradford's decision to move from communal to private ownership at Plymouth Colony illustrates the transition from common to private ownership and the gains that can result. When the land at Plymouth Colony was organized jointly, there was shirking on work and overconsumption of the fruits of the labor even though the group shared common religious values. Communal property rules could not prevent the tragedy of the commons. Bradford reported an unwillingness to work, confusion and discontent, and a prevailing sense of slavery and injustice. In short, the communal experiment was endangering the health of the colony. By dividing the land into individually owned parcels, Bradford provided the colonists with a stronger incentive to work—the fruits of each new landowner's labor would benefit him and his family directly. Property in Plymouth was further privatized in ensuing years when houses and later the cattle were assigned to separate families. According to Governor Bradford, the colony flourished under private ownership, bringing "very good success" (Bethell 1999).

The continuum from communal to private ownership is also demonstrated with Maine's lobster fishery. Lobster fishers have formed community groups known as harbor gangs. These gangs exclude outsiders from the lobster fishery, thus creating an incentive to limit the race to fish. They also monitor who enters the fishery, divide up the fishing territories, and police the territories to ensure that fishers are not encroaching on one another's territories. The success of this system is manifested in higher catches, larger lobsters, and greater incomes for these Maine lobster fishers.

The patent process serves as a modern example of the importance of defining ownership. One of the primary functions of a patent is to convert a commons in idea space into private property, where each inventor defines his or her particular claim (Friedman 2000, 133). Creating rights to ideas gives people an incentive to invent because they have an avenue to exploit their discovery and can ensure that someone else does not enjoy the benefits of the invention without paying for it.

The cost of enforcing property rights defined by patents is constantly changing with new technologies. For example, encryption—a mathematical procedure for scrambling and unscrambling information—makes patented and copyrighted ideas more secure. IBM is developing a digital container called a crytolope that allows access to its information only to those who have paid for it. Because this technology excludes nonpayers, it has been termed "the digital equivalent of barbed wire" (Friedman 2000, 144).

The importance of transferability of property rights must also be emphasized. The ability of the owner to sell his or her assets provides the incentive for efficiency. Consider what allowing transferability of water rights has done to improve water-use efficiency in the American West. Under the *prior appropriation* doctrine, water rights are affirmed by states' giving water users a right to a specified quantity of water. In dry years when not all rights can be met, those with the most senior date of appropriation are allowed to take their water first, followed by the next most senior, and so on (Anderson and Snyder 1997). In states such as Montana, where courts have adjudicated water claims dating back to the nineteenth century, water rights are now well defined and enforced.

Allowing water rights to be transferable is encouraging more efficient and environmentally friendly use. When farmers can sell their water to urban users at a profit, they have an incentive to reduce irrigation by employing superior irrigation technologies or by changing cropping patterns. Urban users save money—water obtained from alternative sources, such as from desalination or damming, costs more.

Private ownership with transferability also illustrates how gains from trade can create strange bedfellows. The Rainey Wildlife Sanctuary is 27,000 acres of marsh in Louisiana owned by the Audubon Society and managed for the benefit of the species it protects. Not only does the society own the land, it owns the mineral rights, in particular, the oil and gas rights (Snyder and Shaw 1995). What distinguishes Rainey from federal sanctuaries is the coexistence of wildlife and oil-drilling operations. There were tradeoffs for the Audubon Society between preserving the pristine sanctuary and earning royalties from the energy resources, but the society minimized the impact on the sanctuary by requiring special drilling techniques and equipment. As John Mitchell put it in an article in *Audubon* magazine (1981), the sanctuary's manager, David Reed, "liked the idea of cooperating with industry in a situation where it was likely there would be no adverse impact on the biotic community."

Government Regulations

Perhaps the most frequent response to the tragedy of the commons today, though not necessarily the most effective or the most common historically, is governmental regulation (see De Alessi 2003 and Yandle 2003). Government regulation can save resources from extinction and reduce conflict by restricting people from access to the commons and by enforcing the restrictions.

Consider government regulation of oyster beds in Maryland (De Alessi 1975, 2000). The state government regulates the season, the size of the oysters that can be collected, the daily catch, and the harvesting techniques that are allowed. It enforces regulations by patrolling with boats and helicopters and by placing inspectors at landing stations. The state also helps sustain the resource by fertilizing the oyster beds with oyster shells during the off-season.

Similarly, states regulate hunting to prevent other species from suffering the fate of passenger pigeons. As with oyster harvesting, states regulate seasons, set bag limits, and prescribe hunting methods. In some cases, they augment habitat by limiting uses that compete with wildlife and by planting animals and fish in the habitat. State regulation may be necessary because it is costly to establish private property rights to wild animals (see Lueck 2003).

Government regulation to prevent the tragedy of the commons, however, is no panacea for several reasons. First, enforcement of restrictions on access is costly. Regulatory agencies must expend resources monitoring access to the commons and punishing those who violate access rules. In the case of open ocean fisheries, such enforcement costs may be so high that implementation is almost impossible.

Second, as a substitute for high public enforcement costs, regulatory agencies often raise the private cost of taking the resource in an effort to discourage exploitation. In the case of oyster harvesting, for example, Maryland mandated that oyster dredges be pulled by sailboats instead of power boats on certain days of the week. In salmon fisheries, regulatory agencies have limited the size of boats and the types of nets that can be used. These restrictions do increase the costs, but typically do not work as well as we might hope. When smaller boats are mandated, fishers invest in expensive electronic gear for locating fish, thus increasing the productivity of the smaller boats. Agnello and Donnelley (1975a, 1975b) studied oyster beds in sixteen states from 1945 to 1970, finding that average labor productivity was lower on government regulated oyster beds than on privately owned beds. They also found that the privately controlled oyster beds were healthier and produced better quality oysters. Their data show that a shift to private ownership of oyster beds away from public ownership under government regulation increased the average income of oystermen by approximately 50 percent.

Third, even if regulating access to the commons successfully raises the value of the resource, the government will be faced with the problem of who gets access to it. Government regulations can improve game populations, which predictably will attract more hunters. Who should be allowed to hunt the more abundant populations? Limits on open grazing of public lands can improve forage, but who then should have access to the improved forage?

To answer these questions, government will have to allocate access to the valuable rights, and depending on the allocation procedure, people will compete for those rights. Because access to resources is valuable, individuals and firms will invest in trying to bias the distribution system in their favor by using political pressure, campaign contributions, perhaps even bribes. Hence, regulatory agencies can be "captured" by special interest groups. A large body of empirical evidence indicates that government officials often implement policies designed to improve their own welfare by maximizing their power and wealth (see McChesney 1997; Anderson 2000).

Consider government regulation of federal lands that would be subject to the tragedy of the commons if access were not limited. Historically, access has been allocated to miners, loggers, and grazers. More recently, however, the security of this access has been called into question by others who would like to capture the value of environmental amenities from the federal lands. As a result, battles have erupted between competing users of the politically allocated commons, creating a gridlock for land managers (Nelson 1997).

In the case of grazing, for example, environmentalists and ranchers have locked horns. Cattle ranchers have long held grazing permits that give them access to federal lands and allow them to capture some of the value of what would be the commons. Environmentalist argue that the ranchers are getting the permits for fees below what they are worth and that the federal lands should be used to produce amenity values. Nonuse advocates want access for ranchers restricted even further so that they can capture amenity values.

The Arctic National Wildlife Refuge (ANWR)—one of the largest areas in America's wildlife refuge system—provides another example of the problems of political allocation. The ANWR is a region rich in fauna, flora, and oil potential, where development has been debated for more than forty years. Development proponents argue that ANWR oil would help supply America's energy demands and could be done without meaningful harm to the environment. Opponents counter that the ANWR's flora and fauna are more valuable than its oil and therefore any oil found would not provide lasting energy security. The conflict between oil potential and pristine nature is all about who will capture the value of the ANWR. Will it go to developers for energy or to environmentalists for wilderness? Special interest groups have focused on narrow issues, ignoring other costs and forgone opportunities to use or appreciate the land.

In summary, the regulatory approach to resolving the tragedy of the commons simply moves the racing and fighting into the political arena, thus giving government and lawmakers the power to allocate access rights to valuable resources. When property rights are up for grabs in the political arena, would-be demanders will do what it takes to get the attention of politicians and bureaucrats making allocation decisions (see McChesney 2003). Commenting on the problems of government regulation, Nobel laureate Joseph Stiglitz (1993, 599) stated that "government is not some well-intentioned computer that only makes impersonal decisions about what is right for society as a whole. Instead government is a group of people—some elected, some appointed, some hired—who are intertwined in a complex structure of decision making." When governmental solutions are proposed, "it is always appropriate to inquire into not only the extent of the problem, but also whether government can effectively address it."

Property Rights and Economic Growth

When property rights are established and the tragedy of the commons is avoided, cooperation and economic growth prevail. Prosperity follows from freedom because a free society based on secure property rights allows owners to seek and capture the gains from trade inherent in voluntary exchanges. If individuals and businesses do not have secure rights to property and lack confidence that contracts will be enforced and the fruits of their efforts protected, their incentive to engage in productive activity will diminish. In other words, the efficiency of markets follows from secure and tradeable property rights, which are the basis of any truly free society. Hence, property rights are necessary conditions for both freedom and prosperity.

The connection between private property rights, freedom, and economic prosperity has become even clearer since the fall of communism in the Soviet Union and Eastern Europe. Following World War I, many people believed that centrally planned economies could improve on market systems to promote human welfare. The great experiment with communism in the Soviet Union, however, proved that state command-and-control was not a viable alternative to voluntary exchanges between businesses and individuals who own property. The belief that planners could create a better outcome than that produced by individuals directing their privately owned assets was, in the words of Tom Bethell, "the key economic delusion of socialism" (1998, 11). Nobel laureate Friedrich Hayek, in his debates with economic planners following World War II, argued that socialism and communism would put civilization on "the road to serfdom."

Recently, several studies have developed indexes of economic freedom. These indexes differ in some of the variables they include, but they generally measure constitutional enforcement, freedom for contracting, protection of property rights, likelihood of revolutions, and extent of democracy. These indexes compare the level of freedom across countries and over time and estimate the empirical relationship between freedom and economic prosperity.

The conclusion from these studies is unequivocal, namely, economic growth is positively related to the security of property rights. In *The Economic Freedom of the World: 2002 Annual Report* (2002), economists James Gwartney and Robert Lawson found that between 1990 and 2000, nations that scored in the top fifth of the economic freedom rankings had secure property rights. Their average per capita income was US$23,450, and their average economic growth rate was 2.6 percent a year. Nations that scored in the bottom quintile lacked secure property rights, had an average per capita income of US$2,560, and had an average negative economic growth rate of 0.9 percent.

Seth Norton (1998) correlated the extent to which countries have secure property rights with measures of environmental quality and human well-being. In nations where property rights are well protected, Norton found that roughly 93 percent of the population has access to safe drinking water compared with only about 60 percent of the population in countries where property rights are weak. He also found that 93 percent of the population of countries with well-protected rights has access to sewage treatment while in countries without well-protected rights only 48 percent has access to sewage treatment. Norton found similar results when examining life expectancy. Life expectancy is seventy years in countries with strong property rights but only fifty years in countries where property rights are weakly protected. He concludes that "property rights and its related construct, the rule of law, and a more general category, freedom from property rights attenuation, are all positively related to economic growth. Their absence leads to economic stagnation and decline (44)."

Despite the statistical evidence showing the positive relationship between property rights, freedom, and economic prosperity, there has recently been an erosion of property rights in some nations. The Heritage Foundation's 2001 *Index of Economic Freedom* reports that seventeen developing countries have seen a decline in the security of property rights. "What these nations fail to realize," according to the foundation's president, Edwin Feulner, "is that undermining the foundation of one's own prosperity risks bringing about the end of that prosperity, whether through stagnation or economic collapse" (2001, xiv).

Conclusion

The tragedy of the commons can only be eliminated by creating rules for exclusion from the resource in question and by establishing a system to enforce the rules. Often we turn to government regulation as the solution to the tragedy, but government solutions are costly and frequently create new problems. Community ownership is a little-studied way of restricting access to the commons that can work well in small, homogeneous groups. Private property, however, is an alternative for exiting from the tragedy of the commons and provides the potential for substituting cooperation for the conflict inherent in political decisions. If property rights can be defined, enforced, and traded, owners have the incentive to work together and to seek more efficient uses of the resources they own. When clearly specified property rights exist in the context of the rule of law, resources are better cared for, economic prosperity is more likely, and freedom prevails. As Hayek (1973, 107) explains, "The understanding that good fences make good neighbors, that is, that men can use their own knowledge in the pursuit of their own ends without colliding with each other only if clear boundaries can be drawn between their respective domains of free action, is the basis on which all known civilization has grown. . . . Property . . . is the only solution men have yet discovered to the problem of reconciling individual freedom with the absence of conflict."

Of course, the key problem facing any society is how to obtain and maintain such a system of property rights. It is relatively simple to do so for land that can be surveyed and fenced, but it is much more difficult to do so for mobile resources, such as wildlife and air. As we shall see in the next chapter, however, property rights can and will develop given a legal setting that encourages their evolution.

CHAPTER THREE

Where Do Property Rights Come From?

There is nothing which so generally strikes the imagination, and engages the affections of mankind, as the right of property . . . and yet there are very few who give themselves the trouble to consider the origin and foundation of that right.

William Blackstone,
Commentaries on the Laws of England

RETURN TO the scene of two children quarreling over a toy. Such disputes are about property rights—the children are contesting who should control the asset and derive benefits from it. As one says, "It's mine," and the other responds, "No, it's mine," how will the dispute be resolved? Will fighting erupt? Will the parents have to step in and assign the rights? Or will the children resolve the problem through a negotiated agreement?

Not only are these the typical options for the two children, but they also capture the ways that property rights usually evolve in society at large. When two neighbors quarrel about a tree branch that hangs across a fence or the teenager's loud music that disrupts peace and quiet, will they come to a neighborly agreement, will they call the police, or will they come to fisticuffs? When one firm's waste products enter the groundwater and lower water quality in a well used by a neighbor, will the two parties bargain with one another, go to court, or call on the force of government to resolve the issue? When two sovereign nations have a territorial dispute, will they go to war or will they negotiate a treaty to assign borders?

This chapter explores how the evolution of property rights resolves these disputes so that property rights can encourage gains from trade. It focuses on the incentives that children, neighbors, firms, and nations have to peacefully define and enforce property rights and avoid the negative consequences of fighting. Property rights do not just happen; like any other good, they are produced by individuals, groups, and governments who invest in definition and enforcement. As the value of a resource rises or the costs of defining and enforcing property rights fall, or both, people will devote more time and effort to establishing property rights. Whether we are talking about mining claims on the American frontier, patents to new software, or ownership of potential energy supplies in the Arctic, the evolution of property rights is best explained by changes in the costs and benefits of defining and enforcing property rights. This does not mean that well-defined rights will necessarily result whenever two parties have contesting claims to property, but it does mean that disputants have an incentive to hammer out property rights in order to avoid the negative-sum game of war.

Producing Property Rights

If resources are abundant, there is little reason for anyone to quarrel over ownership. When the Lonesome Dove cowboys brought their cattle to fatten on the grasslands of Montana, there was no scarcity of good grazing land, and even when a few other herds arrived, there was no reason to fight. As Ernest Staples Osgood (1929, 182) put it, "There was room enough for all, and when a cattleman rode up some likely valley or across some well-grazed divide and found cattle thereon, he looked elsewhere for range." Similarly with mining camps, the early prospectors moved on when they found someone panning on a stream; it was simply too costly to fight when most likely there were other productive claims. Orbital paths for satellites seemed ubiquitous when Sputnik was first launched. Internet names were not worth fighting over as long as there were only a few users.

But as resources become scarce, the potential for a tragedy of the commons raises its ugly head. This means that overuse can occur and conflicts will arise. Without property rights to the range, overgrazing would result. Without property rights to whales, over-harvesting occurred and continues in many oceans today. People compete for the use of air as a medium through which vistas such as the Grand Canyon can be viewed and into which air pollution can be dumped. Without clear property rights to the use of air, overuse as a dumping medium results. With the increased demand for environmental amenities such as clean air, wildlife habitat, and open space, conflicts over who owns the environment have increased (Hill and Meiners 1998). Can water be diverted for irrigation, or must it stay in the stream for salmon? Can trees be harvested on federal lands, or should those federal lands provide habitat for endangered species?

Each of these examples of increasing scarcity has been met with efforts to resolve the ownership question—who has what rights to use the asset. As a result, access to the commons has been restricted in one way or another. Returning to our example of the fishery, by limiting entry to the fishery, those who obtain the right to fish have an incentive to maintain a sustainable harvest. The resources that would have been wasted in a race to capture the fish (see chapter 2) are saved because those with secure property rights have an incentive to husband the resources.

The genetic structure of living organisms serves as another example of defining ownership over a new frontier. An agreement between Merck & Co. (pharmaceutical products and services) and Costa Rica's National Biodiversity Institute demonstrates the growing cooperation between government and private sector entities to share in the fruits of bioprospecting. In exchange for the right to screen plants and animals being cataloged in Cost Rica, Merck paid some $1.1 million up front, as well as an unspecified percentage of future royalties (American University, Case 47). The contract gave Merck the right to evaluate whether plant, animal, and insect samples might have pharmaceutical and agricultural applications and gave the Costa Rican government an economic incentive to protect its resources.

Economist Harold Demsetz (1967) was the first to point out what now seems obvious, namely, that efforts to define and enforce property rights and hence reduce the waste inherent in the tragedy of the commons will respond to an economic calculus. Demsetz (1967, 334) recognized that "property rights arise when it becomes economic for those affected by externalities [the tragedy of the commons] to internalize benefits and costs." In other words, if the returns from restricting entry exceed the costs, individuals and groups will invest in defining and enforcing property rights.

Exactly how people go about establishing property rights can vary widely depending on the costs and benefits of definition and enforcement. Individuals may rely on social norms that limit behavior—they may post signs, build fences, go to court, or call the police. If the value of the property is low, it might not be worth building a fence, but it might be worth posting a "No Trespassing" sign. Alternatively, if the value of the property is high but the cost of fencing is even higher, guards may be used instead of fences. As we shall see, just as there is no single recipe for baking cookies, there is no single way that property rights will be produced; the best outcome will depend on property rights entrepreneurs.

Property Rights Entrepreneurs

As with the production of all new goods, property rights entrepreneurs are the people who discover innovative ways of establishing ownership. These are the people who see value before others and take action to capture that value. The cattlemen who moved cattle from Texas to Montana and faced the potential of overgrazing established and enforced customary range rights on a first come, first served basis. As the bison were nearly driven to extinction by hide hunters, a few entrepreneurs saw the value of preserving the last few live animals by undertaking the cost of fencing them. Indeed, the bison that remain today are the result of those early property rights entrepreneurs. Today, real estate entrepreneurs incorporate environmental amenities such as streams and open space into their developments, thus establishing ownership of those amenities (Anderson and Leal 1997). In each of these cases, the problem for the entrepreneur is how to establish property rights to capitalize on his or her foresight.

Property rights entrepreneurs are the people who perceive gain for themselves or their group in removing resources from the commons so that they can capture the value of the asset. In doing well for themselves by claiming the resource, property rights entrepreneurs do good for society by eliminating the tragedy of the commons. How much effort they put into definition and enforcement will depend on the benefits and costs.

Benefits of Definition and Enforcement

The main determinant of the benefits to investing in property rights definition and enforcement is the value of the resource in question. If you own an old, beat-up bicycle, investing in an expensive lock to secure your property rights to it probably is not worthwhile. If grazing land is cheap, it will not be worth putting up a fence. If water is abundant, it won't be worth carefully measuring and monitoring how much people use.

As land values rose, cattlemen put increasing effort into defining and enforcing their property rights. Initially they would post signs or publish ads in local newspapers declaring that they had claim to a certain range. As the number of cattlemen increased, they formed cattlemen's associations that declared the range closed and banned together to exclude outsiders. They hired cowboys to live in "line camps"—cabins that were located on the boundary line between ranges—and patrol the perimeter of their range.

Land values still have an impact on the amount of effort put into defining and enforcing property rights. Though almost all land is surveyed, the exact boundary line is usually less precise between two large parcels in Montana than it is between two lots in New York City. When large blocks of land are subdivided, boundaries become more precise because the value per square foot is higher.

As amenity values from land increase, there is more incentive for landowners to clarify their property rights so that they can profit from the increased value (see Anderson and Leal 1997). More and more farmers lease hunting and fishing rights and change traditional agricultural production to enhance wildlife habitat. For example, a housing developer in Boise, Idaho, reclaimed a stream so that it would hold more trout and afford them an improved spawning habitat. He then built houses around the reclaimed stream. This enabled him to capture the value of his investment in the stream through higher home values. A rancher near Bozeman, Montana, who charges a fee for fishing a small stream on his property, has fenced his cattle out of the stream in most places and provided gravel pads where they can drink from the stream so that fish habitat will not be destroyed.

Consider how an increase in the value of oil created an incentive to avoid the tragedy of the commons (see Libecap 2003). Initially, pumpers from an oil pool would race to the pump house to get the oil from a pool before others could. Given the way oil flows, overpumping leaves oil trapped underground and raises the cost of extracting the resource. To overcome the tragedy of the commons, oil companies in Texas called on the state government to help them band together so they could "unitize" oil pools. Unitization defined the perimeter of the pool and coordinated pumping from it in order to eliminate overpumping.

As alternative energy technology improves to allow production from the sun and wind, landowners have more incentive to establish rights to capture those energy sources. As solar panels become more common, rules evolve that specify neighboring building heights so as to optimize everyone's ability to capture the sun. Similarly, those who use wind to generate power do not want airflows disrupted by neighbors, and they will attempt to define their rights to the wind.

These examples illustrate that recognition of new values is only half of the equation; to capture those newly recognized values, property rights entrepreneurs must establish ownership over the relevant assets. In other words, they must invest in the definition and enforcement of new property rights arrangements. Software manufacturers devise codes to prevent people from copying software and thus depriving the software owner of revenues from his product. To protect your right to peace and quiet in your own living room, you can install caller ID to screen unwanted calls. Example after example illustrates how higher values increase definition and enforcement effort.

Working in the opposite direction, lower asset values can induce owners to give up their property rights to those assets. The

best example of this came when the introduction of the tractor
rendered horse power virtually worthless. As a result, unwilling
to retain ownership of horses that had to be fed but served no
purpose, owners turned horses loose on public lands (the basis of
wild horse herds today). In more recent times as railroads have
gone out of business, they have abandoned their rights-of-way.
As new technologies come on line, it may not be worth enforcing
patents to now-obsolete technologies. With all investments, the
willingness of owners to put effort into defining and enforcing
property rights declines as the value of the asset drops.

Cost of Definition and Enforcement

Several factors have an impact on the cost side of the property
rights equation. One of the most obvious is the technology available for defining and enforcing property rights. The invention of
barbed wire is a prime example. Prior to the invention of barbed
wire, with limited supplies of timber for rail fences or stones for
walls, cattlemen depended on the cowboys they hired to defend
the boundary lines between claims.

Responding to the profit opportunity available from providing
a cheaper way to establish and defend boundaries between properties, inventors applied for and received 368 patents for barbed
wire between 1866 and 1868. Ranchers responded by substituting
this inexpensive fencing material for cowboys riding the range,
and in the process made their property rights to land and cattle
more secure. The 80 million pounds sold in 1880 was sufficient to
construct 500,000 miles of fence with four strands of wire, defining
and enforcing property boundaries at a fraction of the cost of
cowboys.

The availability of a low-cost technology for defining and enforcing property rights is just as important today as it was on the
frontier. Satellites and radio tracking devices can better define

and enforce property rights. For example, information gathered by satellites can more precisely define the boundaries on land and sea, and radio tracking devices implanted in migratory species such as whales can identify individual animals. Satellites can also monitor fishing boats so that boats without rights to fish can be excluded from a fishery, and they can track emissions into air and water so that polluters can be accountable for violating the property rights of others (Anderson and Hill 2001). Remote locks on automobiles, motion detectors in backyards, and video cameras are also obvious examples of new technologies that reduce the costs of defining and enforcing property rights and make them more secure.

New opportunities allowing property rights to flourish in the twenty-first century are abundant. Geographic information systems are creating more precise identification and recording of resources so that property rights can be precisely identified. Similarly, isotopes can tag pollutants so that those responsible for polluted emissions can be held accountable for their costs.

Another determinant in the cost of establishing property rights is the physical nature of the resource in question. Property rights to land are more readily defined and enforced because it is possible to survey lines and record boundaries. Mobile resources such as wildlife, water, and air, however, are more difficult to bring under the property rights umbrella. It was much easier to secure ownership, for example, to a dead bison than to a live bison. And because it was easier to enforce property rights to cattle than to bison, it is little wonder that cattlemen encouraged the decimation of bison herds, which competed with cattle for grass. As economist Dean Lueck (1995) explains, when wildlife animals range over wide areas, property rights are less likely to evolve, making government regulation more likely. Hence, the hunting of migratory waterfowl is regulated by international treaties, the hunting of deer is regulated by states, and the hunting of mice is not regulated at all.

The higher costs of defining and enforcing property rights to a mobile resource also manifest themselves in the way water is owned. Once captured and stored, property rights to water can be readily defined, but when it is flowing through time and space, definition and enforcement costs are higher, and when the water flows underground, the costs are higher yet. As a result, groundwater basins are often subject to overpumping, and surface water may be fought over by competing users.

Private Versus Governmental
Definition and Enforcement

As noted at the beginning of the chapter, we generally think that definition and enforcement of property rights is the domain of government, but individuals do have some choice over whether they use governmental or private definition and enforcement. For example, we rely minimally on the government to enforce our rights to our bicycles. In most cases, we do not record the serial number with a government, and we really don't expect the police to enforce our property rights. Instead, most of us rely on private enforcement in the form of strong locks.

Whether people choose private or governmental definition and enforcement depends on the security of property rights provided by the formal legal environment (Yandle 2001). If the legal environment provides inexpensive and secure ways of recording property rights, people are more likely to invest in governmental definition and enforcement processes. Recording a land deed in the county courthouse and registering a car title with the state are important for securing your property rights, and both actions are easy and relatively inexpensive. Even water rights can be made more secure if the state adjudicates conflicting rights, records the settlements, and allows owners to trade their water assets. In this context, common law courts (see chapter 5), which rely on precedent, can enhance the return on defining and enforcing property rights.

On the other hand, when formal legal institutions are lacking or do not provide secure property rights, people are more likely to turn to private definition and enforcement (de Soto 2000). The American frontier provides an interesting historical example. Squatters in advance of formal governmental institutions formed land claims clubs that defined property rights among the members and enforced them against outsiders.

The first cattlemen on the northern plains also organized associations that effectively defined and enforced property rights to land and livestock. They developed customary range rights, posting signs that areas were claimed by members of the association and advertising in local newspapers that ranges were closed to outsiders. For example, a notice published in a Helena, Montana, paper in 1883, asserted:

> We the undersigned, stockgrowers of the above described range, hereby give notice that we consider said range already overstocked; therefore we positively decline allowing any outside parties or any parties locating herds upon this range the use of our corrals, nor will they be permitted to join us on any roundup on the said range from and after this date.

These privately defined and enforced rights were secure enough that they were bought and sold in an active market. Case in point: In 1884, the Swan Land and Cattle Company purchased a 160-acre ranch with improvements and stock from the National Cattle Company for $768,850. Swan also purchased a 320-acre ranch with improvements and cattle for $984,023, and the Valley Land and Cattle Company carried on its books a valuation of $85,000 for the range rights that it owned (see Anderson and Hill

2003). These prices reflect the value of the secure property rights that allowed the owner to restrict entry to the grazing commons. By organizing into regional associations and developing rules for governing property rights, the "cattle community," as historian Ernest Staples Osgood (1929, 115) described it, could achieve three common goals:

> First, to preserve the individual's ownership in his herd and his increase; second, to afford protection to the individual's herds; and third, to control the grazing of the public domain or to prevent overcrowding. These aims, which might have been achieved by an individual in the earlier days of comparative isolation, could now only be realized through group effort.

Early mining camps in the West provide another example of private efforts to define and enforce property rights (see McChesney 2003). Hundreds of miners armed with six-shooters rushing to claim gold had all the potential for conflict and violence, but violence was not the norm. It was "generally confined to a few special categories and did not affect all activities or all people," namely, children, women, and law-abiding citizens. Despite the frontier's reputation for violence, "crimes most common today— robbery, theft, burglary, and rape—were of no great significance. . . ." (McGrath 1984, 247). In 1849, one observer noted that the California mining camps rapidly developed a set of rules that "placed the strong and the weak upon a footing of equality, defined the claims that might be set apart, protected the tools left on the ground as evidence of proprietorship, and permitted the adventurers to hold their rights as securely as if they were guaranteed by a charter from the government" (quoted in Zerbe and Anderson 2001, 115).

Miners also established a new system for defining and enforcing water rights that remains the foundation of water rights in the western United States to this day. In the eastern United

States, where water is relatively abundant and hence diversions (say, for irrigation) are less important, landowners adjacent to streams have riparian rights to an undiminished quantity and quality of water. Thus, upstream users can use water for domestic purposes or power generation, but they cannot divert significant quantities of water or pollute the water so as to sufficiently diminish its quantity or quality for downstream users.

Because the miners had to divert water from streams, first to sluice boxes where gold was separated from gravel and later to hydraulic hoses that provided enough pressure to dislodge gravel-bearing gold from its surrounding geologic structures, they abandoned the riparian system and replaced it with the prior appropriation system (see Lueck 2003). This system granted to the first appropriator an exclusive right to the water and granted to later appropriators rights conditioned on the claims of prior users; minimized the costs of defining and enforcing rights to the fluid resource by requiring diversion and use; and allowed transfer and exchange of water rights among users. Hence, the first pioneers in the West were property rights entrepreneurs by necessity.

In part, cattlemen's associations and mining camps were able to collectively agree on rules for the evolution of property rights because they were relatively homogeneous groups with similar production interests. Cattlemen, for example, had an incentive to band together for roundups on the open range because there were economies of scale. It took many cowboys to round up the cattle twice each year, once in the spring for branding and once in the fall for marketing. If each cattle owner did this on his own, the effort would be replicated several times, but by agreeing on a group roundup, cost savings were significant. Once an association was formed to organize the roundup, it was easier to develop other rules for defining and enforcing property rights.

Today, homeowner and condominium associations provide examples of homogeneous private groups defining and enforcing property rights. With their common purpose, people in associations can limit the types and locations of buildings in subdivisions, self-regulate activities that go on in condominium complexes, and require members to pay dues for providing public goods. As long as groups have a uniform purpose and deal with problems that are confined to the spacial boundaries over which the association has control, private solutions such as these can be effective.

These examples notwithstanding, we primarily rely on government, with its monopoly on the legitimate use of force, to define and enforce property rights. We expect our governments to record and enforce titles to our cars, deeds to our land, and patents to our inventions. Even the early private efforts of cattlemen turned to formal government for implementation of their rules once there were a sufficient number of people to organize governmental units. After cattlemen's associations established private brand registration, for example, they turned to territorial and state governments to codify and enforce brand registration. Similarly, the prior appropriation water doctrine, hammered out in mining camps and irrigation districts, was codified in the earliest territorial and state laws.

Patents and copyrights are another example of the government granting and enforcing property rights to ideas. Imagine what would happen to the brand name Coca-Cola without trademark protection. Without these grants to exclusivity, investment in new ideas, new technologies, and new writings would be less because investors would not be guaranteed the fruits of their labors. Of course, even with state definition and enforcement, property rights cannot be perfectly enforced, as the Napster case, involving reproduction of music on the Internet, illustrates.

At the foundation of governmentally enforced property rights is the Constitution with its limit on the government's ability to take private property without just compensation and due process. If such constitutional constraints are rigidly upheld, people are more likely to invest in private ownership (see chapter 5). In contrast, if they are not, citizens are discouraged from investing in private property. Third World nations, for example, lack the process to represent their property and create capital. As de Soto explains, "They have houses but not titles; crops but not deeds; businesses but not statutes of incorporation" (2000, 7). This helps explain why entrepreneurs have not been able to produce sufficient capital to make domestic capitalism work in the Third World.

Conclusion

After exploring how property rights evolve, it is important to consider whether property rights can devolve. Granting government the legitimate power of coercion necessary to protect private property rights creates a two-edged sword. On the one hand, the state can take advantage of scale economies in enforcement and apply the rules to a broader population, thus providing the basis for economic growth and prosperity. On the other hand, that same coercive power gives government the ability to take private property, a subject we turn to in the next chapter. Paraphrasing Chief Justice John Marshall's ruling regarding the state's power to tax, suffice it to say here that the power to take is the power to destroy.

CHAPTER FOUR

How Secure
Are
Property Rights?

Where an excess of power prevails, property of no sort is duly respected. No man is safe in his opinions, his person, his faculties or his possessions.

James Madison, *Federalist Papers*

SUPPOSE A child is playing with a prized possession and a bully takes it. Most would consider this theft because the bully has no right to take the toy. But suppose that a babysitter, hired by the parents to watch the children and settle disputes, plays favorites and takes a toy that clearly belongs to one child and gives it to another. Because the babysitter is strong and has been granted authority, he or she can transfer the rights, and the child will have to acquiesce, at least until the parents come home. Upon the parents' return, the child can appeal to their high authority to reverse the decision. To prevent future transfers, the child might ask the parents to find a different babysitter and to make it clear to all future babysitters that their actions must be fair.

Such is the problem with the coercive power of government. To enforce property rights and adjudicate disputes, citizens band together to form governments with enough coercive power to implement the rule of law. As discussed in chapter 3, individuals can defend property rights by joining private associations or by exercising their own enforcement activity (locks, fences, alarms). But private definition and enforcement has limitations, providing a rationale for granting government the power to enforce property rights against theft from other citizens and from other nations. The problem then becomes how to prevent the coercive power granted to government from being abused to effect transfers of property.

As the architects of a free society, the United States' Founding Fathers recognized this problem (Siegan 2001). James Madison was particularly concerned about a centralized abuse of power and the security of individual rights. In his speech on December 1, 1829, at the Virginia State Constitutional Convention, he stated, "The essence of government is power; and power, lodged as it must be in human hands, will ever be liable to abuse." Madison frequently expressed his trepidation about the "tyranny of the majority," fearing that majority coalitions in a democracy might vote to take from minorities.

In this chapter, we explore Madison's concerns and how they might be allayed. In order to determine how secure property rights actually are, we look to the structures and outcomes of private enforcement of property rights and compare them with centralized enforcement. After discovering that there can be high costs associated with government's enforcing and defining property rights, we focus on the fundamental dilemma of political economy—how to harness government's coercive power to protect property rights without that power's being used to reallocate rights from one individual or group to another.

Private Versus Governmental Enforcement

Although individuals can enforce their own property rights, there clearly are limits to this approach. The most obvious problem with private enforcement is that if might makes rights, fighting could prevail, consuming valuable resources and destroying the potential for economic progress.

The second problem with individual enforcement is that scale economies can make collective action cheaper and more effective. Just as specialization and scale economies can reduce the cost of producing cars, so can they reduce the costs of enforcement. Up to a point, larger armies can beat smaller armies, which helps explain why we have nation states.

A third drawback to private enforcement is that it can be subject to free rider problems, which arise when those who benefit from certain actions cannot be compelled to pay. When there are scale economies in protecting larger groups, it is difficult to defend only those who pay for protection without securing others in the vicinity. A lock on the door of a house protects just that house and therefore does not provide a free ride for others, but a neighborhood watch program has a deterrent effect for all houses despite the fact that many neighbors do not participate in the program. Even more prone to the free rider problem is protection of a country's borders, which guards all people within those boundaries regardless of whether they have contributed to payment of the cost of such services.

Because private efforts to enforce property rights can be costly and ineffective, individuals form governments, in part, to lower these costs, discourage free riding, and more effectively define and protect rights. To do this, citizens sanction government to be the only legitimate agency with the authority to use coercion for enforcing property rights. David Friedman writes:

> Government is an agency of legitimized coercion. The special characteristic that distinguishes government from other agencies of coercion (such as ordinary criminal gangs) is that most people accept government coercion as normal and proper. The same act that is regarded as coercive when done by a private individual seems legitimate if done by an agent of the government. (1973, 152–154)

In other words, individuals agree to a framework whereby they give government—whether local, state, or national—the authority to coerce themselves or others to provide the public good of law and order. Citizens authorize government to use force legitimately as long as it is used to enhance social welfare.

With its legal monopoly on the legitimate use of force, government can potentially overcome the problems that arise with private definition and enforcement. First, through supplanting the use of force by multiple private parties trying to keep others from violating their property rights, a government can potentially maintain peace among the citizens. Competition among enforcement groups, such as with the Mafia, can lead to a Hobbesian jungle. Similarly, countries torn by civil strife, such as Northern Ireland and Somalia, illustrate what can happen if rules are formed by the might of competing individuals and groups. All sides in these disputes are armed and spend large amounts of time and energy fighting over rights. A single, collectively sanctioned enforcement unit can eliminate this warring competition and replace it with law and order. And when citizens can rely on government for protection, they can focus on productive activity rather than on combat.

Second, government can choose the optimal size police or military force and can take advantage of scale economies where they are available. For local jurisdictions, a smaller unit can patrol and enforce rights against theft. Where jurisdictions overlap, larger units can resolve disputes. For example, county governments can resolve disputes between neighboring towns, state government can resolve disputes between counties, and at the national level, even larger military action can protect citizens from outside threats.

Finally, governments can prevent the free rider problem inherent in the enforcement of property rights. The taxing power allows the government to force would-be free riders to contribute to enforcement and defense, thus overcoming the potential for underprovision by voluntary enforcement groups.

The Trouble with Government

Though there are gains from involving government in the definition and enforcement of property rights, those gains come with costs. One particular problem facing a government trying to give valuable property rights to citizens is that people will find ways of competing to get the property rights. (In New Zealand, this type of competition is called a lolly scramble, referring to a children's party game in which candies are scattered on the floor and children scramble to get their share.)

Consider, for example, land rushes and homesteading. When the federal government made lands on the western frontier of the United States available to those willing to occupy on a first come, first served basis, people could not wait until it was actually profitable to farm the land and market the products; if they waited, someone would be there first. Hence, people competed to get title to the land by racing and enduring a starving time. This explains why failure rates were so high for homesteaders.

The Oklahoma Land Rush in 1893 provides a quintessential example of what can happen when government tries to give away property rights to land. On the morning of September 16, when the Cherokee Strip was to be opened for claiming, between 100,000 and 150,000 people stood ready to race for land. Soldiers with rifles were stationed every 600 yards along the line to prevent "sooners" from starting before the signal. When they did start, bedlam ensued, with horses breaking legs and wagons overturning, the contents strewn across the prairie. People who tried to race on foot were trampled by horses and run over by wagons.

Races still occur if governments try to give away valuable property rights. When public lands are opened for oil or mineral exploration, companies race to establish their claims by exploring. When the U.S. government tried to distribute radio frequencies in the 1930s, people raced to be the first to broadcast on the frequencies and thereby claim a license for that frequency. The racing occurred because frequency assignments were for indefinite periods and based on the principle of first come, first served. Moreover, only a minor background investigation was conducted to establish the need for the frequency (Coase 1962, 40). In Alaska, where overfishing is regulated by limiting the season to a few days, fishers purchase big, powerful boats, race to the best fishing grounds, and catch as many as they can in the short time allowed them.

Moreover, if competition to claim valuable resources being given away by government does not actually cause racing, it still encourages efforts to influence the government's assignment of property rights. The technical term used by economists to describe competition for political property rights is *rent seeking*, where rent is the value of the asset that is up for grabs in the political arena. When a federal agency tries to allocate uses of public lands, for example, the rents from those lands are put up for grabs and competing interest groups try to influence the allocation. The question of whether snowmobiles will be allowed in Yellowstone National Park in the winter months is a case in point. Obviously snowmobilers want to retain the right to ride their machines in the park, and snowmobile manufacturers are more than willing to join in the fight. On the other side are environmentalists who want to preserve the peace and quiet of the park for their enjoyment. Each side spends time and money trying to convince the relevant agencies and Congress that its claim is more meritorious.

Zoning and building regulations are other examples of how the political process can put property rights up for the taking. The property owner who is restricted in the use of his or her property, by, say, the disallowing of commercial development, will see a resulting diminution in the property's value and will fight to prevent such zoning. But a neighboring property owner who will see higher property values because of the restriction will try to get the zoning limitation imposed. The competition is little different from sooners racing to acquire property; parties in the zoning dispute compete by racing to the zoning meeting to make their case.

Astute politicians will attempt to turn these rent-seeking efforts to their favor. Though not common in the United States, corruption would be one way to do this. Campaign contributions, however, offer a legitimate alternative. People who want to get a larger share of the politically allocated pie or prevent their existing share of the pie from being taken away have a substantial incentive to influence politicians through campaign contributions. Thought of this way, politicians are able to get "money for nothing" (McChesney 1997). As long as property rights are allocated and reallocated in the political process, campaign finance reform is unlikely to find much real success.

The Power to Take

Perhaps the biggest problem with governmental enforcement of property rights is that it creates the potential for government to take property rights. Consequently, the fundamental dilemma in establishing government is how to harness coercive power to protect property rights without that power's being used to reallocate rights from one individual or group to another.

Military Takings

The transfer of Indian lands to whites throughout the nineteenth century illustrates how the brute force of government was used to transfer rights (Anderson and McChesney 1994). Despite common perceptions, most of the early history of Indian-white land transactions involved trading rather than taking. In the eastern third of the United States, Indians had relatively well-defined territories within which families and clans had secure property rights to the land they farmed. Combine this with a balance of power and the use of force, and the conditions were right for exchange.

When settlement moved to the West around the middle of the nineteenth century, however, conditions encouraged takings. In the first place, nomadic tribes of the plains had less secure territorial rights and relatively few individual or family rights to land. Given that they depended mostly on migrating buffalo herds for their sustenance, individual land rights made little sense. Secondly, in 1848, because of the Mexican-American War, the United States established a standing army, which dramatically changed the calculus of taking. Especially after the Civil War there were large numbers of troops in the army with little to do. In this setting, the cost of taking fell, and the number of battles over land rights increased dramatically as America's Indian policy shifted from trading to taking.

In the contemporary world, the potential for such takings still disrupts property rights. This problem is obvious in Zimbabwe, where the government of President Robert Mugabe began a program of land reform aimed at redistributing property rights to black citizens in the late 1990s. Black citizens were allowed to squat on private property, thus claiming the land for themselves. Mugabe has been able to use his military to force whites off their land, and by stacking the country's supreme court with his own supporters, he has been able to circumvent constitutional limitations on takings. Not surprisingly, bloodshed has resulted, and the uncertainty of property rights has brought Zimbabwe's economy to a standstill. Similar stories of undefined property rights plague the developing world, where the problem can be accredited to the "electoral advantages of allowing a majority of citizens to dispossess a minority, the very politics of faction that Madison warned about in the Federalist Papers, No. 10" (see McChesney 2003).

Eminent Domain

How can we combat factional behavior and prevent the powers of government from being used to take and redistribute property rights? The framers of the U.S. Constitution were keenly aware of the problems associated with the tyranny of the majority. Madison, in particular, was convinced that in a democracy where majority rules, minority factions were of little threat, but he worried about the potential for democratic majorities to take from minorities.

To be sure, his concerns were well founded, but in today's massive government the potential for special interest reallocating must also be dealt with. In a national setting as large as the United States, voters are often rationally ignorant about what their democratically elected representatives are doing. It is costly to follow every vote taken by senators and congressmen. Also, because most programs concentrate relatively large benefits on one group and diffuse the costs over the entire population, no one really notices the cost of any single program. Hence, politicians can cater to minority special interest groups by redistributing wealth in their favor.

To better understand the implications for property rights, consider the role of the government's power of eminent domain— its ability to acquire property for public use so long as it follows legal procedures and pays just compensation. Recognized public uses for which the power of eminent domain may be used include acquiring land for schools, parks, roads, highways, subways, public buildings, and fire and police stations, to mention a few. A key attribute of eminent domain is that the government can exercise its power to take property even if the owner does not wish to sell his or her property.

When government seeks to acquire land, it usually does so by entering the voluntary market like any other party, but potential sellers may try to get higher than competitive market prices by threatening to hold up the acquisition. Consider, for example, governmental acquisition of land for a highway. If the proposed highway cuts through the land of multiple landowners, any one of the landowners may refuse to sell unless he is paid a higher-than-market-value price. This type of holdout problem provides the rationale for eminent domain power (see Epstein 2003).

Though constrained by the takings clause of the U.S. Constitution (the Fifth Amendment), abuse of eminent domain power can occur because the definition of what constitutes public use is ambiguous. The term *public use* has been interpreted very broadly by the courts. A project need not be actually open to the public to constitute a public use. Instead, generally only a public benefit is required. Suppose, for instance, that a city uses its eminent domain power to acquire property from one business and transfers it to another in the name of redevelopment. Is this a legitimate public good, or is it simply a transfer of property rights from one owner to another?

Several egregious examples were documented by the Castle

Coalition (www.castlecoalition.org 2002) in a report entitled "Government Theft: The Top Ten Abuses of Eminent Domain, 1998–2002." These include an example from New London, Connecticut, wherein a private development organization used the government's eminent domain power to condemn more than a dozen properties, including the home of an eighty-two-year-old woman, to construct an office park. In Marum, Kansas, the city condemned the property of one car dealership to allow a neighboring car dealership to expand. The city of Riviera Beach, Florida, has used its eminent domain power to force 5,000 residents from residential property in order to develop commercial and industrial sites.

An example with a brighter ending comes from Lancaster, California. The Lancaster city council voted to condemn space in a shopping center occupied by a 99 Cents Only store to make room for the expansion of a Costco store. Costco Wholesale Corporation had operated in the mall for a decade before 99 Cents Only opened shop in 1998. Immediately after 99 Cents Only opened, Costco told the city that it needed to expand into the 99 Cents Only space or it might leave the city. In June 2000, city officials voted to condemn the 99 Cents Only store site. The store sued, arguing that the city had violated its Fifth Amendment rights. It won the case when U.S. District Court Judge Stephen V. Wilson blocked any future attempt to take the 99 Cents Only store for private purposes, writing that "the evidence is clear beyond dispute that Lancaster's condemnation efforts rest on nothing more than the desire to achieve the naked transfer from one private party to another. Such conduct amounts to an unconstitutional taking purely for private purposes." In this case, the transfer was stopped, but not without cost to the 99 Cents Only store.

Even without condemnation the potential for regulation diminishes the value of a property. When the Tahoe Regional Planning Agency (TRPA) established zoning rules that prevented Bernadine Suitum from building on her property, the highly valued Tahoe property declined in value. Mrs. Suitum had to go all the way to the U.S. Supreme Court to win the right to even file a lawsuit against the planning agency. The TRPA sought to bypass its constitutional mandate to compensate Mrs. Suitum by giving her "transferable development rights," thinking she could sell these rights to a third party for a portion of the market value. Mrs. Suitum did not want to get involved in the complex scheme; rather, she wanted the TRPA to honor its duty and pay her the compensation she deserved. After six years of litigation, the U.S. Supreme Court ruled in *Suitum v. Tahoe Regional Planning Agency* 520 U.S. 725 (1997) that Mrs. Suitum had a right to be heard by a court and that she was entitled to full compensation for the taking of her property. Though the court ruled in Mrs. Suitum's favor, this case served as a wake-up call to those who thought they were immune from takings.

Richard Epstein (2003) elaborates on the potential for takings in the context of privately inheld lands—private lands surrounded by government lands. Inholders can easily be deprived of the value of their property if the agency controlling the surrounding lands denies access. Easements give the inholder some protection against this type of taking, but with the vagaries of politics, such easements can end up "being an incomplete treaty between two warring tribes" (Epstein 2003). The right of a private inholder to use a government-owned dirt road, for example, creates multiple questions regarding the nature of the entitlement, such as what type of vehicles are allowed on the road or whether the inholder can make repairs to the road and, if so, under what government supervision. As owner of the surrounding land, the government is able to take a portion of the inholder's property value.

The precarious nature of the inholder's rights demonstrates the threats to private property associated with the government's ownership of land. This scenario has been played out frequently on property in the western United States, where numerous inholdings exist and where environmental groups are pressuring government to acquire additional public lands. As this acquisition increases, the conflict between public and private ownership increases the likelihood that government coercion will result in the factional tyranny that Madison feared.

To make the takings problem worse, it is often difficult to determine what constitutes just compensation given that land is not homogeneous. The object of compensation is to put the owner of the publicly acquired property "in as good a position pecuniarily as if his property had not been taken" (*Olsen v. United States* 292 U.S. 264, 1934). If eminent domain procedures worked perfectly, the amount of compensation given to the private property owner would be set at a level where the private property owner would be indifferent between the land he held and the payment he received. Interpretations of takings law, however, frequently ignore this fundamental concept by refusing to compensate for the total amount of loss resulting from government action. This result, according to Epstein (2003), "leads to profound allocative distortions: The lower prices stipulated by the government lead to an excessive level of takings, which in turn increases the size of government relative to what it should be, and thereby alters for the worse the balance between public and private control."

Conclusion

Government can play a positive role in defining and enforcing private property rights. It can maintain law and order, lower the overall cost of this protection, and eliminate the free rider problem in providing protection. Doing so requires that government have coercive power, which in turn creates a double-edged sword. The same coercive power that protects private property can be used to take private property, especially if done in the name of the public's safety and welfare. As explained in the introduction to the *Economic Freedom of the World* report (Fraser Institute 1996):

> The fundamental function of government is the protection of private property and the provision of a stable infrastructure for a voluntary exchange system. When a government fails to protect private property, takes property itself without full compensation, or establishes restrictions that limit voluntary exchange, it violates the economic freedom of its citizens.

It might be possible to reduce the potential for such violations by not allowing the government to acquire any property at all, but this would require sacrificing benefits that may come from governmental ownership. The obvious example would be military property, but others include administration buildings, historic monuments that may have intrinsic preservation value, and public highways where private toll roads are infeasible. Nonetheless, by more carefully limiting the purposes for which governmental property can be acquired, the potential for uncompensated or undercompensated takings could be reduced.

A stricter interpretation of the takings clause of the U.S. Constitution provides another potential limit on governmental takings of private property. As Madison realized, judicial review can provide "an impenetrable bulwark against every assumption of power in the Legislative or Executive" (Annals of Congress 457, 1789). As we have seen over the years, however, it is one thing to assert that judicial review will provide this bulwark, and another for the courts to strictly interpret the takings clause.

The remaining question, addressed in chapter 5, is whether or not the protection of property rights can be maintained to promote continued prosperity. The modern property rights movement is fueled by the belief that property rights in the United

States are being eroded in favor of legislated and regulated controls. If so, what are the prospects for reestablishing the sanctity of property rights necessary for ensuring freedom and continued improvements in human welfare and progress?

CHAPTER FIVE

Will
Property Rights
Be Preserved?

Let the people have property and they will have power—a
power that will forever be exerted to prevent the restriction
of the press, the abolition of trial by jury, or the abridgment
of many other privileges.

Noah Webster,
The Founder's Constitution

OUR EXAMPLES featuring children at the beginning of each
chapter illustrate the importance of rules to civil play. For board
games, written rules become a type of constitution that governs
play. When children are inventing a game as they play it, they
hammer out new rules as disputes arise. They have to work together to decide what rules are fair, and they may ultimately have
to appeal to the "supreme court," in the form of parents. When
children cannot agree on the rules, their play may break down
completely, in which case they disband and lose the value of play.
Such negative-sum results give children an incentive to find ways
to cooperate. Ultimately, even if rules are written and clear, co-

operation depends on a shared set of values about what is right and what is fair.

So it is with the future of property rights in a civil society. No matter how well specified the property rights, anarchy may prevail if people do not share a belief in the property rights system. As we will see, constitutions, federalism, and common law all contribute to the sanctity of property rights, but ultimately, adherence to the rules requires that the populace believes in limited government and respects the rights of others.

From Defense to Erosion

In each of the two freedom indexes mentioned in chapter 2, the United States ranks high, although not at the top. The United States is currently ranked number four in the Heritage Foundation's 2002 index and three in the Gwartney and Lawson 2002 index. The United States enjoys considerable security of property rights, especially when compared with other countries around the world. But compared with the sanctity of property rights at the time of the nation's founding, erosion has undoubtedly occurred.

The Founding Fathers took seriously their business of preserving liberty through the protection of property rights (see Anderson and Hill 1980 for a more complete discussion of what follows). As Irving Kristol (1975, 39) put it, the political activity unleashed by the Revolution "took the form of constitution-making, above all." In their debates over ratification of the Constitution, the Federalists recognized that "In framing a government which is to be administered by men over men, the great difficulty lies in this: you must first enable the government to control the governed; and in the next place oblige it to control itself." They were clear in the Fifth Amendment of the Bill of Rights that no person should "be deprived of life, liberty, or property without due process of law."

With the Constitution ratified, the next step was implementation and interpretation, which again reflected the founders' belief that protecting property rights was paramount to the success of their experiment. No other justice of the Supreme Court has been more forceful in protecting property rights than Chief Justice John Marshall. Using the contract clause, the commerce clause, and the Fifth Amendment, he continually fortified barriers against takings. In his dissent in *Ogden v. Saunders* 25 U.S. 213 (1827), the only case in which he was in the minority, Marshall revealed his Lockean values and defended the right to contract on the grounds that it "results from the right which every man retains, to acquire property, to dispose of that property according to his own judgment, and to pledge himself for a future act. These rights are not given by society, but are brought to it." The Constitution's protection of property rights for the seventy-five years after ratification led historian James Willard Hurst to characterize the period as a "release of energy."

By the last quarter of the nineteenth century, however, the barriers erected by the Founding Fathers in the Constitution and Bill of Rights were beginning to break down. Much of the erosion came in the form of regulations found to be constitutional as long as they were "reasonable" and in the "public interest"—two vague terms that gave regulators substantial latitude. In a dissenting opinion in one of the most famous regulation cases, *Munn v. Illinois* 94 U.S. 113 (1877), Associate Justice Stephen Field said, "If this be sound law, if there be no protection, either in the principles upon which our republican government is founded, or in the prohibitions of the Constitution against such invasion of private rights, all property and all business in the State are held at the mercy of the majority of its legislature." Historian John W. Burgess (1923) concluded that until the end of the nineteenth century, constitutional interpretations "had been an almost unbroken march in the direction of more and more perfect individual liberty and immunity against the powers of government, and a more and more complete and efficient organization and operation of sovereignty back of both government and defining and guaranteeing individual liberty." Thereafter, however, he believed that the movement had been "in the contrary direction, until now there remains hardly an individual immunity against governmental power which may not be set aside by government, at its own will and discretion, with or without reason, as government itself may determine."

Modern Breakdown

One area in which the breakdown of property rights has accelerated over the past fifty years is environmental regulations. The Endangered Species Act (ESA) of 1973, for example, specifically precluded the taking of a listed species, meaning intentionally shooting, trapping, or harming an endangered animal or harvesting an endangered plant. Because ownership of wild animals in the United States has always resided with federal and state governments, few questioned these regulations in the beginning. The word *harm*, however, was interpreted by the U.S. Fish and Wildlife Service to include habitat modification on private and public lands, and through court rulings, harm was defined more and more broadly. Eventually, habitat modification that did not harm a specific animal or plant but had the potential to do so was interpreted to constitute a taking of an endangered species and therefore caused the land to be subject to regulation.

Not surprisingly, *habitat* became a word that landowners dreaded hearing. Listed species on private land brought with them the prospect of financial penalties and restrictions on land use. A family in Riverside County, California, for example, was denied the right to plough its land and was threatened with a fine of $50,000 and a year in prison if it did so because the area was habitat for the endangered kangaroo rat. In another case, land-owner Ben Cone was prevented from harvesting old growth pine on his property because it was home to the red-cockaded wood-peckers. As a result of the regulation, Cone began harvesting trees at forty years of age rather than eighty in order to preclude the trees from growing old enough to provide woodpecker habitat. Because landowners consider regulations under the Endangered Species Act to be takings, such regulations create perverse incentives that pit landowners against species. As the landowner in the Riverside County example put it, the regulations "have placed ourselves and the species and habitats in adversarial roles" (Bethell 1998, 305).

Wetlands legislation serves as another example of an environmental measure that sparked a nationwide movement to protest against government encroachments on private uses of property. The Clean Water Act of 1972 was stretched to cover mudflats, prairie potholes, and large puddles. Eventually, lands could be classified as wetlands even if they were dry for 365 days of the year. Federal jurisdiction, according to Bethell, "was claimed in ways that could have been written by the satirist of *Saturday Night Live*. Prairie potholes could affect interstate commerce, it was argued, because geese flying from one state to another could glance down and spot a waterhole—the 'glancing geese' test" (Bethell 1998, 306). Law-abiding citizens could be sent to jail for filling in ditches on their own land.

An additional area where regulation went wild was in urban renewal projects. Throughout the 1950s and 1960s, federal financing provided the means to condemn hundreds of "slum" neighborhoods across the country, then resell the land at bargain prices to private developers. Those who were being forced out of their neighborhoods were to be relocated to "safe and sanitary housing." The regulation ended up destroying five times as many low-income housing units as it created, and in the end the blight was far worse than what had originally existed. *Time* magazine acknowledged in 1987 that urban renewal was a "well-intended and wrong-headed federal mission" that had the effect of tearing down "densly interwoven neighborhoods of nineteenth- and early-twentieth-century low-rise buildings and putting up expensive, charmless clots of high-rises. Or even worse, leaving empty tracts" (quoted in Bethell 1998, 300). Urban renewal regulation replaced property rights with political control. What the regulators didn't realize was that all along it was property rights that protected poor neighborhoods through the direct incentive of private property owners to ensure that their properties are well maintained for potential buyers. Private owners will always have the motivation to manage property better than a room full of urban planners. The unsuccessful program was discontinued in 1973. The most important consequence of these regulatory contrivances has been a new push to rebuild the barriers to property rights.

Rebuilding the Barriers

From the Magna Carta to the present, people have struggled to create governments that are strong enough to protect property rights, but that are prevented from taking property rights without due process and just compensation. The challenge we continue to face is little different from that of the Founding Fathers— namely, how can property rights be protected from taking by individuals and by government? To rebuild the barriers against property rights takings, we must resurrect constitutional limita-tions, encourage federalism that devolves governmental authority to lower levels that are more accountable, and rely more on com-mon law than on regulations for resolving property rights ques-tions.

Resurrecting Constitutional Barriers

Prior to ratification of the U.S. Constitution, many states frequently violated citizens' property rights by authorizing such projects as the building of roads across private property without compensating the owner (Siegan 2001). In order to protect liberties, specific restraints on federal and state powers were created in the Constitution. The value of property rights was well understood by the framers, who viewed property rights as undeniable rights of human beings that are critical to maintaining life, liberty, and the pursuit of happiness. Consequently, they created the Fifth Amendment as the primary barrier for the protection of property rights.

Bruce Yandle (1995, xii) has described the Fifth Amendment to the U.S. Constitution as America's chief property rights wall. This wall preserves resources and allows government and liberty to coexist while enabling a society to prosper and flourish. In order to keep this wall from crumbling, however, new mortar must be applied when cracks appear. Property rights advocates often look to the courts to act as the mortar. In many ways, according to Yandle, "property rights advocates are calling for a modern-day Magna Carta." Once again, ordinary people are seeking to contain government. But instead of having to settle differences with picks and swords, the struggle resides in the courts and legislative bodies (Yandle 1995, xi).

The primary protection of property rights in the United States rests on the interpretation of the Constitution by the courts. Heavy regulations throughout the 1970s, such as the ESA, sparked a nationwide movement of protest against government encroachment on private uses of land, which included a shift by the Supreme Court toward greater protection of property rights. Consider two landmark cases, *Lucas v. South Carolina Coastal Council*

505 U.S. 1003 (1992) and *Dolan v. City of Tigard* 512 U.S. 687 (1994). Petitioner Lucas bought two residential lots on a South Carolina barrier island for nearly $1 million, intending to build homes similar to those on the adjacent parcels of land. Two years after Lucas purchased the lots, the state legislature enacted the Beachfront Management Act, which barred Lucas from building on his parcels. He filed suit, contending that the ban on construction deprived him of all "economically viable use" of his property and therefore effected a taking under the Fifth and Fourteenth Amendments. The Supreme Court decided in favor of Lucas, and the Coastal Council eventually paid Lucas $1.5 million for his property.

The Dolan case involved the owner of a plumbing supply business in Oregon. City authorities refused to allow the owner to enlarge her store unless she set aside 10 percent of her land for use as a bicycle path and a greenway. The Supreme Court ruled that the town should have purchased the land rather than held it hostage. Both of these cases helped reverse a trend developing since the 1930s of approving various government infringements on the rights of individuals in the name of the public interest. In these cases, the Supreme Court helped place property rights back on the same level with the individual rights protected by the First Amendment (Pipes 1999, 252).

Fortifying Federalism

Court decisions are not the only way to protect property rights and keep government from roaming too far from its Constitutional borders; government can be reined in by reinforcing the concept of federalism. President Reagan (Executive Order 12612, 1987) defined federalism by saying it "is rooted in the knowledge that our political liberties are best assured by limiting the size and scope of the national government." As Bruce Yandle (2001b) explains, "Federalism and property go hand in hand" because federalism delegates authority for producing public goods to the most efficient level of government. For example, if noise levels from one person adversely affect the peace and quiet of another, the conflict can be dealt with by local government to the extent that the noise in question does not spill over to residents of other governmental jurisdictions. Hence, noise ordinances are typically implemented by city councils. However, because the noise from jet aircraft taking off and landing is not confined to the airport and its immediate vicinity, noise standards may be dealt with at a higher level of government, such as county or state.

Economist David Haddock (1997, 16–17) summarizes how we can think about the optimal level of federalism. There are benefits to centralizing governmental functions. These include taking advantage of scale economies, enforcing property rights against other citizens and noncitizens, and bringing all third-party effects (for example, air, water, and noise pollution) under a single regulatory unit. But "pointing to the benefits while ignoring concurrent costs is inappropriate, for ideal regulation would maximize net rather than gross benefits." In other words, we should consider how large the scale economies are and how widespread the third-party effects are. It is entirely possible that capturing the benefits of either of these will be exhausted before regulation becomes national. Moreover, there are the costs of monitoring regulatory performance, which grow, perhaps exponentially, as we move from local to state to national regulation. Haddock concludes that "Many of the gross benefits could be preserved through properly devolved regulations, while substantial costs could be avoided."

Efficiency in governmental action promoted by accountability is another benefit of federalism. With administrative actions delegated to the lowest political denominator, a connection between benefits and costs of governmental procedures is more transparent. This in turn helps limit the size and scope of government.

Consider the decision of a governmental body to obtain land for a public park. The taking power of the government allows it to condemn the property and pay just compensation, but is this worth doing? If the benefits from the public park accrue to the local community and if payment for the property must come from local taxes, decision makers will have more incentive to carefully weigh the benefits and costs of providing the park. Suppose, however, that the local park is provided by a higher level of government that can diffuse the costs of paying for the land over a wider group of citizens, many of whom get no benefits from the park. In this scenario, local interest groups have an incentive to lobby for more parks than they otherwise would because they do not bear all the cost. Moreover, if the costs are sufficiently diffused, the taxpayer will likely be poorly informed about the costs and benefits. If so, it is more likely that the government will convert private to public property when the benefits of doing so may not warrant it (see Epstein 2003).

When made at the local level, governmental decisions to acquire property rights are further constrained by the ability of people to "vote with their feet" (see Fischel 2003). If a community takes property without compensation or even raises taxes to pay for acquiring property that is not worth the costs, citizens can move to communities that more carefully weigh benefits and costs. If the acquisition (with or without compensation) is done at higher levels of government, however, the citizen who believes that the government is not being fiscally responsible has few options. In other words, as the potential for voting with one's feet declines, the potential for taking and for inefficient acquisitions increases. Communist countries surrounded by fences during the Cold War provide an example of what can happen when federalism is disallowed and migration is restricted. In this setting the potential for taking property and freedom is virtually without limit.

Relying More on Common Law

In chapter 3, we discussed the evolution of property rights, noting that people facing the tragedy of the commons have an incentive to escape the tragedy by defining and enforcing property rights. Hence, cattlemen formed associations to limit grazing on the open range, miners and farmers established water rights to allocate the precious resources in the arid West, and lobster fishers used local associations to limit entry into the fishery. In each of these cases, the potential for an efficient evolution of property rights was driven by the the players' having a stake in finding a workable solution to the commons problem.

Though examples of these types of private definition and enforcement efforts are less prevalent today, common law provides a way for property rights to evolve from the bottom up. Common law is judge-made law, which exists and applies to a group on the basis of historical legal precedents developed over hundreds of years. Common law resolves disputes between competing users of a resource who bring their contested uses before a court. For example, if one person dumps her effluent into a stream from which another person takes his domestic and livestock water, there is a conflict over which party has the right to use the stream for his or her respective purpose. Either the two parties must bargain out of court to resolve their differences or go to court for resolution. In court, each party will try to make the case that it has the right to use the stream for its particular use and that the violation of rights caused it harm. Whenever possible, the court will rely on precedent to give continuity to the evolution process and in reaching a decision will establish further precedent for who has what right.

Consider the case in New York of *Whalen v. Union Bag & Paper Co.* 208 NY 1 (Ct.App., NY 1913). A new pulp mill that created hundreds of jobs polluted a creek used by Whalen, a downstream farmer. The court awarded damages to Whalen and granted an injunction against Union Bag to stop the damage-causing pollution within a year. In its ruling, the court emphasized that Whalen had property rights that could not be violated and that there was precedent for enforcing his rights. In its decision, the court found that

> The fact that the appellant has expended a large sum of money in the construction of its plant, and that it conducts its business in a careful manner and without malice, can make no difference in its rights to the stream. Before locating the plant, the owners were bound to know that every riparian proprietor is entitled to have the waters of the stream that washes his land come to it without obstruction, diversion, or corruption . . . .

Such rulings were typical of common law courts resolving property rights disputes and provided precedent upon which future users of streams could decide whether they could conduct their business "without injury to their neighbors." Karol Ceplo and Bruce Yandle (1997, 246) conclude that resolving property rights disputes in this way "meant there was no excuse for uninvited pollution that significantly reduced water quality. To avoid water rights litigation, polluters could have contracted with riparian rights from downstream landowners or bought all the land along the stream. This was, in fact, common practice."

Because litigation is a negative-sum game in which one party's loss is the other party's gain and both parties to the dispute will bear costs in the fight, each has an incentive to minimize the cost of settlement (see Haddock 2003). For this reason, a majority of disputes are settled out of court. When disputes do go to court, it is because the rights are so unclear that both parties believe they have a strong case that their rights were violated.

The common law process has several benefits with regard to protecting property rights, as Yandle notes:

> [T]he common law emerges on a case-by-case basis from real controversies adjudicated by common law judges. Common law evolves in a small-numbers setting. Through judges' traditional use of precedents in deciding cases, the law is generalized to a large number. . . . The common law process is continuous; an opportunity for modification and the introduction of new knowledge is afforded each time a common law judge writes an opinion. (2001b, 11)

In short, the common law approach to the evolution of property rights provides continuity, precedent, stability, and efficiency.

Contrast the common law approach to resolving conflicts over property rights with the statutory or regulatory approach. The statutory approach has two types of costs. First, regulations seldom promote efficiency because neither the costs nor the benefits are borne directly by the parties contesting resource use. Return to the zoning example. If one individual or group can down-zone another individual's property and if the down-zoned property owner has no recourse (either compensation or voting with his feet), there is little reason to expect that the reduced value of the down-zoned property is offset by the increased value of the other property. In other words, zoning regulations offer the potential of a free lunch for some at the expense of others, and if people can get free lunches, they have no incentive to ask whether the meal is worth the cost.

Second, regulations cause rent seeking. Recall that rent seeking refers to the time and money that individuals or groups invest in the political process to prevent their property from being taken or to get someone else's property redistributed to the rent seeker. Because the regulatory approach puts property rights up for grabs, it encourages the same type of race that resulted from homestead-ing. As we saw in the case of the homestead acts, there was more effort expended in wasteful rent seeking when the process of defining and enforcing property rights process was dictated from the top down. People who fear that their property rights will be taken through regulations will invest in protecting their rights, and people who think they can get those rights will invest in trying to influence the regulations in their favor.

Decisions about the use of public lands illustrate the rent-seeking costs inherent in the regulatory process. Traditionally, federal lands have been used for commodity production such as logging, grazing, and mining. As the demand for amenity values has risen since the 1970s, however, environmental groups have lobbied to get federal lands managed for their purposes. In many instances, this has resulted in a management gridlock (Anderson 1997). Environmental regulations generally, including endan-gered species, clean air, clean water, and land use policy, illustrate how pervasive regulatory rent seeking can be (Anderson 2000). As Jonathan Adler (2000, 25) states, "As long as environmental decisions made in Washington have the potential to reallocate billions of dollars from one set of interests to another, those interests will be sure that they have their say." To make matters worse, the billions of dollars are continually put up for grabs, in each legislative session, adding to the rent-seeking cost and mak-ing property rights all the less secure.

Beyond Formal Barriers

Although institutional barriers such as constitutions, federalism, and common law are the bulwark of property rights protection, these formal institutions have little effect if people do not believe in limited government and the sanctity of property rights. All of the written rules that one can imagine will not thwart powerful leaders and their followers from usurping legitimate rights. Indeed, property rights institutions were generally cast aside during the hundred-year experiment with communism. And President Mugabe's tyrannical reign in Zimbabwe, as noted previously, provides a classic case of a leader supposedly elected in a democratic vote and constrained by a constitution that explicitly protects property rights riding roughshod over private property owners. Explicit rules protecting property rights may be a necessary condition for preserving their sanctity, but such rules are not sufficient in and of themselves.

Ultimately, protecting property rights requires a populace that understands the importance of this institution, that recognizes that limited government is a necessary condition for protecting private ownership, and that is willing to elect political agents who are willing to defend property rights. This understanding has waxed and waned since the drafting of the Constitution.

One indication that an appreciation of property rights is currently on the rise is the number of states enacting laws to protect private property rights. In 2001, twenty-three states had passed laws requiring their governments to assess whether governmental actions constituted a taking of property rights and to compensate when this was the case. Even at the national level, Congress has considered various bills that would require assessments and compensation similar to state laws. None of the national bills have passed, but the fact that they are being considered is evidence of a heightened awareness of the current fragility of property rights.

Some developing countries are also showing signs of implementing the lessons of property rights. Examples include: the creation of land titles for farmers in Thailand, which has led to reduced forest destruction; the assignment of property titles to slum-dwellers in Indonesia, which has tripled investment in sanitation facilities; and the establishment of a security of tenure for farmers in Kenya, which has dramatically reduced soil erosion.

Furthermore, a plethora of recent cases has illustrated the point that local institutions will have a greater sense of responsibility for stewardship. Decentralization of management responsibilities to local groups or private parties, such as the forest user groups in Nepal, has resulted in rehabilitation of degraded lands, planting of new forests, and improved forest management efforts. Effective and lasting methods are being devised all over the world to maintain sustainable resource flows. The mechanisms share the critical features of clear ownership rights and responsibilities, which introduce the economic incentives for stakeholders to create and implement solutions that are sustainable over the long term.

Conclusion

Many of the most important conflicts among today's political systems are over property. How much property can the state tax or take away? Should individuals be able to accumulate wealth without limit, or should estate taxes control the amount that can be accumulated and passed on? What counts as intellectual property? These types of questions provoke important philosophic, legal, and political debate, on which we have touched. We have presented some of the basic intellectual foundations regarding what property rights are, how they work, how they evolve, and how they can be protected.

In the end, the sanctity of property rights depends on a populace committed to a limited, decentralized government and to respecting the rights of others. We have made great progress over the past fifty years in guaranteeing civil rights, but we have failed to make the connection between civil rights and property rights. The former can only exist if the latter are secure. As the court declared in *Lynch v. Household Finance Corp.* 405 U.S. 538 (1972): "Property does not have rights. People have rights. . . . In fact, a fundamental interdependence exists between the personal right to liberty, and the personal right in property. Neither could have meaning without the other." Property rights are civil rights. Only through vigorous protection of property rights can we maintain a truly free and just society.

John Adams (*A Defense of the American Constitutions*, 1787) claimed that "[t]he moment that idea is admitted into society that property is not as sacred as the laws of God, and that there is not a force of law and public justice to protect it, anarchy and tyranny commence. Property must be sacred or liberty cannot exist." The rise in the number of laws explicitly requiring government to assess the impacts of its regulations on private property and to compensate is a good sign. But explicit laws will only be effective if we have the will to defend property rights. With that will also come freedom and prosperity.

REFERENCES

Adler, Jonathan. 2000. Clean politics, dirty profits: Rent seeking behind the green curtain. In *Political Environmentalism: Going Behind the Green Curtain*, edited by Terry L. Anderson. Stanford, Calif.: Hoover Press.

———. 2002. Property damage: A supreme retreat on the protection of private property rights. *National Review Online* (May 1) [online]. Available: www.nationalreview.com.

Agnello, Richard J., and Lawrence P. Donnelley. 1975a. Prices and property rights in the fisheries. *Southern Economics Journal* 42 (2): 253–62.

———. 1975b. Property rights and efficiency in the oyster industry. *Journal of Law and Economics* 18 (2): 521–34.

American University. 2002. *Merck-Inbio Plant Agreement: Case Number 47* [online]. Available: www.american.edu.

Anderson, Terry L. 1995. *Sovereign Nations or Reservations? An Economic History of American Indians*. San Francisco: Pacific Research Institute.

———. 1996. Conservation Native American style. *PERC Policy Series* PS-6. Bozeman, Mont.: Political Economy Research Center.

———. 1997. *Breaking the Environmental Policy Gridlock*. Stanford, Calif.: Hoover Press.

————, ed. 2000. *Political Environmentalism: Going Behind the Green Curtain*. Stanford, Calif.: Hoover Press.

Anderson, Terry L., and Peter J. Hill. 1980. *The Birth of a Transfer Society*. Stanford, Calif.: Hoover Press.

————, eds. 2001. *The Technology of Property Rights*. Lanham, Md.: Rowman and Littlefield Publishers, Inc.

————. 2003. The evolution of property rights. In *Property Rights: Cooperation, Conflict, and Law,* edited by Terry L. Anderson and Fred S. McChesney. Princeton, N.J.: Princeton University Press, forthcoming.

Anderson, Terry L., and Donald R. Leal. 1997. *Enviro-Capitalists: Doing Good While Doing Well*. Lanham, Md.: Rowman and Littlefield Publishers, Inc.

————. 2001. *Free Market Environmentalism*. New York: Palgrave.

Anderson, Terry L., and Fred S. McChesney. 1994. Raid or trade: The economics of Indian-White relations. *Journal of Law and Economics* 37 (April).

————, eds. 2003. *Property Rights: Cooperation, Conflict, and Law*. Princeton, N.J.: Princeton University Press, forthcoming.

Anderson, Terry L., and Pamela Snyder. 1997. *Water Markets: Priming the Invisible Pump*. Washington, D.C.: Cato Institute.

Aristotle. 1984. *Politics*, translated by Carnes Lord. Chicago: University of Chicago Press.

Bethell, Tom. 1998. *The Noblest Triumph: Property and Prosperity Through the Ages*. New York: St. Martins Press.

Bethell, Tom. 1999. How private property saved the pilgrims. In *Hoover Digest: Research and Opinion on Public Policy 1999 No. 1*. Stanford, Calif.: Hoover Press.

Blackstone, William. 1766. *Commentaries on the Laws of England*. Vol. 2. Oxford: Clarendon Press.

Bowen, Catherine Drinker. 1966. *Miracle at Philadelphia*. Boston: Little, Brown and Company.

Burgess, John W. 1923. *Recent Changes in American Constitutional Theories*. New York: Columbia University Press.

Castle Coalition. 2002. Government theft: The top ten abuses of eminent domain, 1998–2002 [online]. Available: www.castlecoalition.org.

Ceplo, Karol, and Bruce Yandle. 1997. Western states and environmental federalism: An examination of institutional viability. In *Environmental Federalism*, edited by Terry L. Anderson and Peter J. Hill. Lanham, Md.: Rowman and Littlefield Publishers, Inc.

Coase, Ronald. 1962. The interdepartment radio advisory committee. *Journal of Law and Economics* 5:17–47.

De Alessi, Louis. 1975. The economics of regulation in the oyster industry. Washington, D.C.: Department of Economics, George Washington University.

———. 1980. The economics of property rights: A review of the evidence. *Research in Law and Economics* 2:1–47.

———. 2003. Gains from private property: The empirical evidence. In *Property Rights: Cooperation, Conflict, and Law,* edited by Terry L. Anderson and Fred S. McChesney. Princeton, N.J.: Princeton University Press, forthcoming.

De Alessi, Michael. 1999. Resource conservation and private management solutions. Paper presented at the Third International Lobster Congress (September), Australia.

———. 2000. Fishing for solutions: The state of the world's fisheries. In *Earth Report 2000: Revisiting the True State of the Planet*, edited by Ronald Bailey. New York: McGraw-Hill.

De Soto, Hernando. 2000. *The Mystery of Capital: Why Capitalism Triumphs in the West and Fails Everywhere Else*. New York: Basic Books.

Demsetz, Harold. 1967. Toward a theory of property rights. *American Economic Review* 57 (2): 347–59.

Eggertsson, Thráinn. 2003. Open access versus common property. In *Property Rights: Cooperation, Conflict, and Law,* edited by Terry L. Anderson and Fred S. McChesney. Princeton, N.J.: Princeton University Press, forthcoming.

Epstein, Richard A. 2000. *Liberty, Property, and the Law: Private and Common Property.* New York: Garland Publishing, Inc.

———. 2003. In and out of public solution: The hidden perils of forced and unforced property transfer. In *Property Rights: Cooperation, Conflict, and Law,* edited by Terry L. Anderson and Fred S. McChesney. Princeton, N.J.: Princeton University Press, forthcoming.

Fischel, William A. 2003. Public goods and property rights: Of Coase, Tiebout, and just compensation. In *Property Rights: Cooperation, Conflict, and Law,* edited by Terry L. Anderson and Fred S. McChesney. Princeton, N.J.: Princeton University Press, forthcoming.

Friedman, David D. 1973. *The Machinery of Freedom.* New York: Harper Colophon.

———. 2000. *Law's Order: What Economics Has to Do with Law and Why It Matters.* Princeton: Princeton University Press.

Gordon, H. Scott. 1954. The economic theory of a common property resource: The fishery. *Journal of Political Economy.* 62 (2): 124–142.

Gwartney, James, and Robert Lawson. 2002. *The Economic Freedom of the World: 2002 Annual Report.* Vancouver: Fraser Institute.

Haddock, David D. 1997. Sizing up sovereigns: Federal systems, their origin, their decline, their prospects. In *Environmental Federalism*, edited by Terry L. Anderson and Peter J. Hill. Lanham, Md: Rowman and Littlefield Publishers, Inc.

———. 2003. Force, threat, negotiation: The private enforcements of rights. In *Property Rights: Cooperation, Conflict, and Law,* edited by Terry L. Anderson and Fred S. McChesney. Princeton, N.J.: Princeton University Press, forthcoming.

Hardin, Garrett. 1968. The tragedy of the commons. *Science* 162:1243–48.

Hayek, Friedrich A. 1973. *Law, Legislation and Liberty, Vol. I: Rules and Order.* Chicago: University of Chicago Press.

Hill, Peter J., and Roger Meiners, eds. 1998. *Who Owns the Environment?* Lanham, Md.: Rowman and Littlefield Publishers, Inc.

Hobbes, Thomas. [1651] 1985. *Leviathan.* Reprint, London: Penguin Books Ltd.

Huffman, James L. 1992. An exploratory essay on Native Americans and environmentalism. *University of Colorado Law Review* 63 (4): 901–920.

Hume, David. 1778. *The History of England.* Vol. 1. London: T. Caddell.

Kristol, Irving. 1975. The American Revolution as a successful revolution. In *The American Revolution: Three Views.* New York: American Brands.

Libecap, Gary D. 2003. Contracting for property rights. In *Property Rights: Cooperation, Conflict, and Law,* edited by Terry L. Anderson and Fred S. McChesney. Princeton, N.J.: Princeton University Press, forthcoming.

Lueck, Dean. 1995. The economic organization of wildlife institutions. In *Wildlife in the Marketplace,* edited by Terry L. Anderson and Peter J. Hill. Lanham, Md.: Rowman and Littlefield Publishers, Inc.

———. 2003. First possession as the basis of property. In *Property Rights: Cooperation, Conflict, and Law,* edited by Terry L.

Anderson and Fred S. McChesney. Princeton, N.J.: Princeton University Press, forthcoming.

Madison, James. 1792. Federalist papers. In *The Papers of James Madison*, edited by William T. Hutchinson et al. Chicago: University of Chicago Press.

Martin, Paul S. 1984. Prehistoric overkill: The global model. In *Quaternary Extinctions*, edited by Paul S. Martin and Richard G. Klein. Tucson: University of Arizona.

McChesney, Fred S. 1997. *Money for Nothing*. Cambridge: Harvard University Press.

———. 2003. Government as definer of property rights: Tragedy exiting the commons? In *Property Rights: Cooperation, Conflict, and Law,* edited by Terry L. Anderson and Fred S. McChesney. Princeton, N.J.: Princeton University Press, forthcoming.

McGrath, Roger D. 1984. *Gunfighters, Highwaymen and Vigilantes*. Berkeley: University of California Press.

Megginson, William, Robert Nash, and Matthias van Randenborgh. 1996. The record on privatization. *Journal of Applied Corporate Finance* 9 (spring): 403–52.

Mitchell, John G. 1981. The oil below. *Audubon* 83 (May): 16–17.

Muir-Leresche, Kay, and Robert Nelson. 2000. *Private Property Rights to Wildlife: The Southern Africa Experiment*. Washington, D.C.: Competitive Enterprise Institute.

Nelson, Robert. 1997. *Public Land, Private Rights*. Lanham, Md.: Rowman and Littlefield Publishers, Inc.

Norton, Seth. 1998. Property rights, the environment, and economic well-being. In *Who Owns the Environment?* edited by Peter J. Hill and Roger E. Meiners. Lanham, Md.: Rowman and Littlefield Publishers, Inc.

O'Driscoll, Gerald P., Jr., Kim R. Holmes, and Melanie Kirkpatrick. 2001. *Index of Economic Freedom.* Washington, D.C.: Heritage Foundation and *Wall Street Journal.*

O'Driscoll, Gerald P., Jr., Kim R. Holmes, and Mary Anastasia O'Grady. 2002. *Index of Economic Freedom.* Washington, D.C.: Heritage Foundation and *Wall Street Journal.*

Osgood, Ernest Staples. 1929. *The Day of the Cattleman.* Minneapolis: University of Minnesota Press.

Ostrom, Elinor. 1990. *Governing the Commons.* New York: Cambridge University Press.

Pipes, Richard. 1999. *Property and Freedom.* New York: Vintage Books.

Rand, Ayn. 1964. *The Virtue of Selfishness.* New York: The New American Library, Inc.

Runte, Alfred. 1990. *Trains of Discovery.* Niwot, Colo.: Roberts Rinehart.

Siegan, Bernard H. 2001. *Property Rights: From Magna Carta to the Fourteenth Amendment.* New Brunswick, N.J.: Social Philosophy and Policy Foundation and Transaction Publishers.

Snyder, Pamela, and Jane Shaw. 1995. PC oil drilling in a wildlife refuge. *Wall Street Journal,* 7 September, A14.

Sowell, Thomas. 1982. *Knowledge and Decisions.* New York: Basic Books.

———. 2001. *Basic Economics: A Citizen's Guide to the Economy.* New York: Basic Books.

Stiglitz, Jospeh E. 1993. *Economics.* New York: W. W. Norton & Co.

Stix, Gary. 2002. Who owns you? *Scientific American* (March) [online]. Available: www.sciam.com.

Webster, Noah. 1787. An examination into the leading principles of the federal Constitution. In *The Founders Constitution.* Chicago: University of Chicago Press.

Yandle, Bruce, ed. 1995. *Land Rights: The 1990s' Property Rights*

Rebellion. Lanham, Md.: Rowman & Littlefield Publishers, Inc.

———. 2001a. Legal foundations for evolving property rights technologies. In *The Technology of Property Rights*, edited by Terry L. Anderson and Peter J. Hill. Lanham, Md.: Rowman and Littlefield Publishers, Inc.

———. 2001b. Federalism: Power and property. In *Federalist Government in Principle and Practice*, edited by Don Racheter and Richard Wagner. New York: Kluwer Academic Publishers.

———. 2003. Property rights or externalities? In *Property Rights: Cooperation, Conflict, and Law,* edited by Terry L. Anderson and Fred S. McChesney. Princeton, N.J.: Princeton University Press, forthcoming.

Zerbe, Richard O., Jr., and C. Leigh Anderson. 2001. Culture and fairness in the development of institutions in the California gold fields. *Journal of Economic History* 61 (March): 114–43.

INDEX

ABOUT THE AUTHORS

TERRY L. ANDERSON is the Martin and Illie Anderson Senior Fellow at the Hoover Institution. Anderson also serves as executive director of the Political Economy Research Center (PERC) and is a professor emeritus of economics at Montana State University, both in Bozeman, Montana. He is the author or editor of twenty-four books, including *Free Market Environmentalism*, coauthored with Donald Leal, and *The Not-So-Wild Wild West* with Peter J. Hill. Anderson's work has helped launch the idea of free market environmentalism to encourage the stewardship of resources and market incentives to spur conservation and protection of the environment.

LAURA E. HUGGINS is a research fellow at the Hoover Institution, where she is currently conducting research for a book on population policy entitled *Population Bomb: Myth or Reality?* Prior to arriving at the Hoover Institution, Huggins served as a graduate fellow at PERC, where she wrote *Reforming State Parks by Moving Toward Self-Sufficiency: A Practical Guide*. Huggins also worked at the Institute of Political Economy, where she published "Innovative Government" in *Controlling Costs by Contracting Services*. She is primarily interested in the role of economic processes in shaping natural resource policy and in promoting market principles to a wide audience in order to help resolve environmental dilemmas.